T0196164

Other Books by Bradley W. Rasch

1. *Psychology: The Important Stuff*
2. *Extreme Trivia: The Chicago Professional Sports Trivia They Do Not Want You to Know*
3. *Explaining and Defending American Government*
4. *Extreme Presidential Trivia: Little Known Facts about Our Presidents*

THE
GOVERNORS
OF ILLINOIS
AND THE
MAYORS
OF CHICAGO

PEOPLE OF REGIONAL, NATIONAL, AND INTERNATIONAL CONSEQUENCE

BRADLEY W. RASCH

iUniverse, Inc.
Bloomington

The Governors of Illinois and the Mayors of Chicago
People of Regional, National, and Inrternational Consequence

iUniverse books may be ordered through booksellers or by contacting:

iUniverse
1663 Liberty Drive
Bloomington, IN 47403
www.iuniverse.com
1-800-Authors (1-800-288-4677)

ISBN: 978-1-4759-6303-8 (hc)
ISBN: 978-1-4759-6304-5 (sc)
ISBN: 978-1-4759-6302-1 (e)

Library of Congress Control Number: 2012921855

Printed in the United States of America

iUniverse rev. date: 11/13/2012

Dedication

To Illinois's best political science instructor: Emily Jansen.

CONTENTS

PART TWO THE MAYORS OF CHICAGO

2. Political science students at the university level.

The framers of Illinois's current constitution did not allow for term limits for Illinois governors. They say that ignorance is bliss. Were the writers of the state's constitution giddily happy, or did they see prison as being the institution that provided for gubernatorial term limits? Mayors of Chicago can also serve unlimited terms. Is the mayoral office one of hereditary entitlement?

3. The casual reader and history buff.

This book is presented in an interesting and readable style. Those who enjoy biographies, history, or politics will find this book entertaining and informative.

All kidding aside, let's take a look at these interesting and (for the most part) decent public servants.

PART ONE
The Governors of Illinois

Shadrach Bond (1818–1822)

Edward Coles (1822–1826)

Ninian Edwards (1826–1830)

John Reynolds (1830–1834)

William Lee Davidson Ewing (1834)

Joseph Duncan (1834–1838)

Thomas Carlin (1838–1842)

Thomas Ford (1842–1846)

Augustus Chaflin French (1846–1853)

Joel Aldrich Matteson (1853–1857)

William Henry Bissell (1857–1860)

John Wood (1860–1861)

Richard Yates (1861–1865)

Richard James Oglesby (1865–1869)

John McAuley Palmer (1869–1873)

Richard James Oglesby (1873)

John Lourie Beveridge (1873–1877)

Shelby Moore Cullom (1877–1883)

John Marshall Hamilton (1883–1885)

Richard James Oglesby (1885–1889)

Joseph Wilson Fifer (1889–1893)

John Peter Altgeld (1893–1897)

John Riley Tanner (1897–1901)

Richard Yates (1901–1905)

Charles Samuel Deneen (1905–1913)

Edward Fitzsimmons Dunne (1913–1917)

Frank Orren Lowden (1917–1921)

Lennington Small (1921–1929)

Louis Lincoln Emmerson (1929–1933)

Henry Horner (1933–1940)

John Henry Stelle (1940–1941)

Dwight Herbert Green (1941–1949)

Adlai Ewing Stevenson (1949–1953)

William Grant Stratton (1953–1961)

Otto Kerner Jr. (1961–1968)

Samuel Harvey Shapiro (1968–1969)

Richard Buell Ogilvie (1969–1973)

Daniel Walker (1973–1977)

James Robert Thompson (1977–1991)

James Edgar (1991–1999)

George Homer Ryan (1999–2003)

Rod Blagojevich (2003–2009)

Pat Quinn (2009–Present)

1

SHADRACH BOND
1818–1822

How many Illinois residents know that their first governor was named Shadrach? Not many, I'd wager. Shadrach's brothers were named Joshua and Nicodemus. All the Bond boys had biblical names.

Bond moved to Illinois and lived and farmed with his uncle, also named Shadrach Bond (What are the odds?).

Bond was a serious farmer and was an advocate for improving the conditions of farm families.

Before coming to Illinois, when living in the Indiana territory, he was a member of the General Assembly and served one term in Congress. When in Congress, he pushed for a law that would allow settlers in Illinois to obtain clear title to the land they had worked. This law led to massive immigration to Illinois.

Bond is most noted for his overseeing the smooth transition of Illinois from a territory to a state.

Long after serving as governor, he was appointed registrar of the land office in Kaskaskia. He held this position until the day he died.

Shadrach was seen as a man of integrity and had a commanding presence. He was rather tall and stocky.

He viewed himself primarily as a farmer, not a politician.

Shadrach Bond's major contribution: He oversaw Illinois's transition from a territory to a state.

2

EDWARD COLES
1822–1826

The second governor of Illinois was an abolitionist long before that was fashionable. He was the son of John Coles, a slaveholder and prominent military figure in the American Revolutionary War. Coles grew up on his father's plantation in Virginia. When growing up, he met Madison, Monroe, and Jefferson through his father. Coles's father was Patrick Henry's father-in-law.

When Coles was twenty-three, he inherited his father's plantation in Virginia. For a brief time, he served as private secretary to President Madison. This was an important and prestigious position in the early days of our republic.

He traveled to Illinois after selling his father's plantation, freeing his slaves while he was in transit.

He soon ran for governor in Illinois as an antislavery candidate. Two proslavery candidates split the proslavery vote, which allowed Coles to win the governorship with far less than a majority.

After serving as governor, he made a great deal of money from real estate investments in St. Louis. He retired to Philadelphia and enjoyed a good deal of traveling in his retirement years.

Coles County (home to Eastern Illinois University) was named after Governor Coles.

Edward Coles's major contribution: He had the courage to be an antislavery politician before taking such a stance was popular.

3

NINIAN EDWARDS
1826–1830

And you thought Rod Blagojevich had an unusual name. We may have discovered a pattern of unique names here.

First came Shadrach, and then Ninian. Should Rod Blagojevich have been that much of a surprise?

Ninian's name may not have served him well politically, but he did have great political and governmental experience.

Before moving to Illinois, while a resident of Kentucky, he was a member of that state's House of Representatives and held various judgeships in Kentucky, culminating in his serving as Kentucky's Supreme Court chief justice.

In Illinois, he served as the last territorial governor, as a US senator (twice, each time as a member of a different political party), and as the nation's minister to Mexico.

Edwards was a slaveholder and an advocate of slavery.

As territorial and state governor, Edwards, as commander-in-chief, twice ordered Indian removal by the state militia.

Edwards was governor when Illinois was expanding greatly.

After serving as governor (Illinois governors were limited by the state constitution to one term), he ran for Congress and lost.

After leaving politics, he dedicated himself to charitable work, working with people who were ill.

One of Edwards's sons served as secretary of the treasury for Abraham Lincoln. Another founded the famous brokerage firm AG Edwards.

Edwards authorized the construction of Illinois's first penitentiary, an institution that would become home to several future Illinois governors.

Edwards has both a town and a county in Illinois named after him.

Ninian Edwards's main contribution: He governed Illinois during a period of rapid growth. He distinguished himself in his post-political career by being very active in medical charity work.

4

JOHN REYNOLDS
1830–1834

It is fair to portray Governor Reynolds as a career politician and public servant. He was one of the original Supreme Court justices for the state of Illinois. Additionally, he was elected to the Illinois House of Representatives, where he served as Speaker of the House. After serving as governor of Illinois, he served several terms in the US House of Representatives.

Edwards was a scout during the War of 1812 and worked as an attorney when he was a young man. He learned French, believing that French was the proper language for a gentleman to use.

He could not get enough of politics. After serving as governor, he ran unsuccessfully for both the State Senate and state superintendent of schools.

The most interesting fact about Governor Reynolds was his war service. In 1832, while serving as governor, he put on the uniform of the state militia and led the troops in the Black Hawk War.

John Reynolds's main contribution: He set an example that public service is important, having always sought to serve in some capacity, even when the office and responsibilities were less than those of positions he previously held.

5

WILLIAM LEE DAVIDSON EWING
1834

Such a long name, he served such a short time.

His first entry into public life, after having practiced law, was when President James Monroe appointed him Receiver of the Land Office in Vandalia, Illinois, in 1820. He also was a general in the state militia, a clerk in the State House of Representatives, a member of the State House of Representatives (where he became Speaker of the State House), a member of the State Senate (where he served as president pro tempore), and acting lieutenant governor. Ewing served as governor of Illinois for only fifteen days, because he was appointed to fill out Senator Elias Kane's term, who died in office.

Ewing was not reelected to the US Senate. He returned to the Illinois House, where he was again chosen as Speaker. At the time of his death, he was serving as Illinois Auditor of Public Accounts.

William Ewing's major contributions: None. He did not really serve as governor long enough to have an impact.

6

JOSEPH DUNCAN
1834–1838

Like many politicians, Governor Duncan had a military resume. He served his country as a soldier during the War of 1812 as well as during the Black Hawk War.

His political bona fides included a stint in the Illinois House of Representatives from 1825 to 1829. He also served as a US congressman.

Governor Duncan served from 1834 to 1838. He ran again for governor in 1842 but lost.

Duncan was quite the builder and developer. He worked hard to pass the Internal Improvements Act, which led to many roads, highways, bridges, and canals being built in Illinois. These improvements modernized and advanced the state but also led to crushing debt. The interest on this debt was massive and problematic. The debt accrued was not paid off until 1882 and hampered state expenditures for some time. This debt nearly led to the state's bankruptcy. To the governor's credit, once he realized the debt service would be so high, he tried to stop his grand development plan, but the legislature insisted on seeing it through.

Under Governor Duncan, the state capital was moved from Vandalia to Springfield. A young representative pushed for this move so hard that he was considered a bully. The efforts of this strong-willed legislator led to a term being coined for political bullying: "log rolling." The legislator was Abraham Lincoln.

Joseph Duncan's major contributions: He oversaw massive infrastructure development and moving the state capital to Springfield.

7

THOMAS CARLIN
1838–1842

Governor Carlin was not extensively formally educated, but he was an avid learner and reader throughout his life. He was a military man, as were so many of Illinois's governors, having served in both the War of 1812 and the Black Hawk War.

He served in the Illinois House for two terms and then spent two terms in the Illinois Senate. President Andrew Jackson appointed him as Receiver of Public Monies in Quincy, Illinois, a post that gave him sufficient public notice for him to be elected Illinois's seventh governor from 1838 to 1842.

Carlin oversaw an overhaul of the state's judiciary system, expanding the Illinois Supreme Court by five judges.

During Carlin's tenure, the Mormons founded Nauvoo and Chicago began to take its place as an important American city. The Illinois-Michigan Canal was also constructed.

After serving as governor, Carlin briefly served again in the Illinois House of Representatives.

After leaving politics, Carlin returned to farming.

The Illinois city of Carlinville was named in his honor.

Thomas Carlin's main contributions: The expansion of the judiciary, the Illinois-Michigan Canal, and his military service.

8

THOMAS FORD
1842–1846

Governor Ford was not a vampire, but he did graduate from Transylvania University. He was not a shark, but practiced law.

As was the case with many public officials, he served in the military (in the Black Hawk War).

Ford's legal career led to a life in politics. He served as a state's attorney and then as a circuit court judge. He eventually also served as a judge in the Chicago Municipal Court and as an Illinois Supreme Court justice. It was his legal career that prepared him to serve as Illinois's eighth governor.

The Illinois-Michigan Canal was completed during Governor Ford's term, and he established canal tolls to help lessen the state's fiscal deficits.

Ford ordered the Illinois State Militia to Nauvoo to deal with the strife between the Mormons and non-Mormons.

After retiring from public service, he returned to the practice of law and wrote a book on the history of Illinois.

Thomas Ford's major contributions: The completion of the Illinois-Michigan Canal, and the use of tolls on that canal to help with the state's fiscal difficulties.

9

AUGUSTUS CHAFLIN FRENCH
1846–1853

Illinois's ninth governor overcame some significant challenges in his life. His father passed away when he was quite young, and his mother died when he was only nineteen. He attended a prestigious school, Dartmouth, but was unable to finish because of his financial limitations. He had a very successful legal career in Illinois (at the time, law school graduation was not a prerequisite for becoming a lawyer) and was a member of the Illinois legislature for two years. He served as Receiver of Public Monies and as a member of the Electoral College—all this before being elected governor.

A lot happened during French's tenure: A new state constitution was developed, the Illinois Central Railroad was completed, the state's fiscal deficit was eliminated, and the Mormons that remained in Illinois emigrated from the state.

After serving as governor, French, like many governors before him, led a very productive public life. He taught law and served as a bank commissioner.

Augustus French's main contributions: He put Illinois's fiscal house in order, a new constitution was developed, and the Illinois Central Railroad was completed. As a man that lost both parents at a young age, he accomplished a great deal.

French was reelected due to a change in the state constitution.

10

JOEL ALDRICH MATTESON
1853–1857

Before coming to Illinois, Joel Matteson was a hands-on kind of guy. He was a businessman and an educator, and he even worked as a foreman, building the first railroad in the state of South Carolina. He continued his labors in Illinois, working as a general contractor on the Illinois-Michigan Canal.

Politically, he got his start as a three-term state senator and then became governor. Aldrich was a very popular governor.

After serving as governor, he ran for a US Senate seat and lost.

After that, his name was linked to a scandal involving monies spent on the canal. He ceded property worth a quarter of a million dollars to the state (a great deal of money at the time) to indemnify himself, never admitting guilt. In retirement, he was the president of the Illinois and Alton Railroad.

A southern suburb of Chicago, Matteson, was named in his honor.

Joel Matteson's main contributions: He made it possible for businesspeople to be considered for high office and indemnified his name before being linked to a possible scandal.

11

WILLIAM HENRY BISSELL
1857–1860

Governor Bissell holds the distinction of being the first Republican governor of Illinois. He practiced both medicine and law before entering politics. After moving to Illinois, he worked as a prosecutor and served as a colonel during the Mexican-American War.

His entry into politics began when he was a Democratic US congressman. He switched parties before running for governor.

When he was in Congress, he had a heated exchange with Jefferson Davis. Davis challenged him to a duel but backed down.

Bissell died in office.

William Bissell's major accomplishment: He was Illinois's first Republican governor.

12

JOHN WOOD
1860–1861

John Wood was a very accomplished man with a very patriotic pedigree. His father was a prominent officer and surgeon during the Revolutionary War. He himself was one of five Illinoisans sent to Washington, DC, to work on a peace conference, the purpose of which was to avoid the American Civil War.

Wood was a state representative and lieutenant governor before becoming governor. He served as William Bissell's lieutenant governor. He served out Governor Bissell's term after he died in office. Wood did not run for reelection in his own right.

His successor, Governor Yates, named him to serve as Illinois quartermaster general, equipping Illinois soldiers who served in the Civil War. He later served as a high-ranking officer during the war.

A community college was named after Wood.

John Wood's greatest accomplishment: Serving so well in many important capacities.

13

RICHARD YATES
1861–1865

Yates began his political career as a representative to the Illinois General Assembly and then went to Washington to represent Illinois in Congress. A strong antislavery advocate, he was against the Kansas-Nebraska Act, which promoted slavery to some degree. Yates was a strong Lincoln supporter on the national level and a nationally prominent antislavery figure.

After serving as Illinois's "War Governor" during the Civil War, he was elected to the US Senate.

Yates died in 1873 while inspecting railway construction in Arkansas for President Grant.

Richard Yates's most important accomplishments: He was a major antislavery voice nationally and saw Illinois through the Civil War.

His son also became governor.

14

RICHARD JAMES OGLESBY
1865–1869

Like many other Illinois governors, Oglesby served the state as both governor and US senator.

He had a very compelling life story: an orphan at a young age, he became a farmer, a lawyer, a gold prospector (he was a forty-niner), and an officer in the Mexican-American War.

His first foray into politics (running for Congress) resulted in defeat in 1848. He was successful for a State Senate bid in 1861 but resigned his seat in Springfield to serve in the Union Army as a colonel during the Civil War. He eventually became a major general and was wounded in the war's last battle. Seriously injured, he resigned his commission. He became Illinois's fourteenth governor in 1865.

Governors could not succeed themselves in those days, so he waited until 1872 and was elected governor a second time. The state legislature then elected him to serve in Washington to represent Illinois as a US senator (there was no direct election of senators by the people in these times), so Oglesby resigned as governor and was sworn in as a senator.

After serving in the US Senate, he was elected governor of Illinois a third time in 1885.

After his last term as governor ended in 1889, he quietly retired to private life.

Richard Oglesby's major contributions: A compelling life story, a "man for all seasons," and a national reputation as a patriot and decent public servant. A true American hero.

15

JOHN MCAULEY PALMER
1869–1873

Illinois's fifteenth governor was an enigma of sorts. Master politician or man of conscience? Independent or flip-flopper?

Palmer had an impressive resume. He had a military background and also served as a US senator, as have so many of Illinois's governors.

Palmer worked as an attorney and also taught the law. He had a blue-collar background of sorts, working as a schoolteacher and a clockmaker. In his early political life, he was a probate judge and served at the Illinois 1847 State Constitutional Convention.

As he forayed into partisan politics, he served as the president of Illinois's first Republican State Convention. He also represented Illinois at the National Republican Convention.

Palmer soon gained valuable experience at the state and national levels. He served as a member of the Electoral College, as a member of the National Peace Conference (the committee charged with the responsibility of trying to avoid civil war), and as a general in the army during the Civil War.

He then became Illinois governor, succeeding Richard Oglesby and then being succeeded by the same man.

Palmer frequently switched parties as he ran for various offices, and he once ran for president of the United States as a member of the Sound Money Party. He received no electoral votes.

Before he died, he published his autobiography, *The Story of an Earnest Life*.

He died in 1900.

John Palmer's greatest accomplishments: He was "his own man." He changed parties at will and stated, "I thought for myself and [have] spoken my own words on all occasions."

16

RICHARD JAMES OGLESBY
1873

This time, Oglesby served only ten days, resigning to become a US senator. The republicans ran him for governor intending to name him to the senate.

17

JOHN LOURIE BEVERIDGE
1873–1877

When young, he planned for a career as a clergyman but practiced law and taught. He served during the Civil War, eventually rising to the rank of general.

After the Civil War, he worked in the sheriff's department in Cook County; was elected to the Illinois State Senate, the US Congress, and the US Senate (resigning to become Illinois lieutenant governor); and then succeeded Governor Oglesby as governor of Illinois.

After Beveridge served as Illinois's seventeenth governor, President Chester Arthur appointed him US Treasurer for the Chicago area.

Beveridge died in 1910, and his grave can be viewed in Chicago's famous Rosehill Cemetery, where many notable people have been interred.

John Beveridge's greatest accomplishments: All in all, a fairly unremarkable administration, but an impressive war record.

18

SHELBY MOORE CULLOM
1877–1883

Governor Cullom was a very accomplished man, also serving as a US senator, as have many of his fellow Illinois governors.

Cullom's professional life began with teaching and the practice of law. He also served as a city attorney.

Cullom served as a presidential elector in the Electoral College and as a member of the Illinois General Assembly, where he eventually became Speaker of the House.

President Lincoln appointed Cullom as a member of the War Claims Commission. He was also a delegate to the National Republican Convention.

After serving as governor, Cullom was elected to the US Senate, where he had a long and distinguished career.

Cullom also was appointed by President McKinley to a commission investigating the conditions in the Hawaiian Islands.

Shelby Cullom's major contributions: Successful tenure as governor, a distinguished career as a US senator, and a national reputation for integrity. He had a long and successful career as a public servant.

19

JOHN MARSHALL HAMILTON
1883–1885

John Marshall Hamilton served as a private during the Civil War. After the war he attended Ohio Wesleyan University and became a teacher. He eventually became a professor of Latin at Illinois Wesleyan University. Hamilton studied law, was admitted to the bar in 1870, and became a practicing attorney in Bloomington, Illinois. His first foray into politics began in the Illinois State Senate, followed by service as Illinois's lieutenant governor. Hamilton became governor when Governor Cullom resigned to serve in the US Senate.

During his term as governor, compulsory education was mandated in Illinois and liquor licenses became required.

Hamilton became a prominent Chicago-based attorney after his governorship.

John Hamilton's major contribution: He is credited as serving when compulsory education was codified.

20

RICHARD JAMES OGLESBY
1885–1889

Oglesby served his third term as Illinois's governor. Remember, at this time, the Illinois constitution did not allow a governor to succeed himself, but it did allow him to serve multiple terms.

21

JOSEPH WILSON FIFER
1889–1893

Governor Fifer also served as an enlisted man during the American Civil War and was seriously wounded in that conflict. His professional career, like so many others politicians, started in the field of law. He served as an attorney for Bloomington, Illinois, and as a state's attorney.

Fifer served two terms in the Illinois State Senate and then became Illinois's twenty-first governor.

A number of important changes occurred when Fifer was in office. The most notable was allowing women to vote for school officers in all elections. Public school law was codified during Fifer's term, and the direct election of US senators began.

After his gubernatorial career, he served several years on the nation's Interstate Commerce Commission and was a delegate to Illinois's 1920 Constitutional Convention.

Joseph Fifer's major contributions: They may well have been partial female suffrage during his term, as well as his service on the national stage after his governorship.

22

JOHN PETER ALTGELD
1893–1897

Despite being born in Germany, Altgeld too was a Civil War veteran. He also served as a private.

After the war, he began the practice of law and spent time as a prosecutor in Missouri. When he moved to Illinois, he was a judge in Cook County.

Altgeld was a very progressive Democratic governor. He oversaw the development of a state home for juvenile offenders, pardoned some of the Hay Market rioters (because he did not feel that they had received a fair trial), and toughened child labor laws. His progressive stances may have kept him from winning a subsequent term as governor.

Altgeld had one last foray into politics: he ran for mayor of Chicago and lost.

In retirement, his progressive days were not over. He authored the book *Our Penal Machinery and Its Victims.*

John Altgeld's major contribution: He was a very progressive governor. Arguably, this may have hurt his electability with some of Illinois's voters.

23

JOHN RILEY TANNER
1897–1901

Governor Tanner was the state's first twentieth-century chief executive.

Tanner was one of several Illinois governors who served as a private during the Civil War. After the war, he served as Clay County sheriff and clerk of the circuit court; he was an Illinois state senator, a US Marshal, the state's treasurer, a railroad commissioner, and an assistant US Treasurer for Chicago. He then went on to become governor.

With his impressive fiscal experience, he emphasized putting the state on good financial ground and eliminated the state's deficit.

After serving as governor, he engaged in a hard-fought campaign for the US Senate and lost. This loss took a toll on his health.

During Tanner's tenure, he used the state's militia to quell rioters during a coal miners' strike.

The Allen Bill, which gave control of Chicago's transportation network to controversial financier Charles Yerkes, was enacted during Tanner's gubernatorial term.

John Tanner's major contribution: He utilized his fiscal expertise well in putting the state's finances in order.

24

RICHARD YATES
1901–1905

Richard Yates Jr. was the son of Illinois's thirteenth governor.

This Yates graduated from the University of Michigan Law School and practiced law in Jacksonville, Illinois. He was a prominent journalist and editor in Jacksonville.

Yates began his career as a public servant by working as the city attorney for Jacksonville. He then served as a judge in Morgan County and a collector of revenue for the United States out of the Springfield office.

Governor Yates made some courageous decisions. He vetoed a bill that would have allowed for horse racing. More importantly, he mobilized the state militia to protect black citizens during some severe race riots in Saline County.

Yates ran two more times for the governorship but did not win either time. Not finished with public service, he became a public utilities commissioner and was the state's assistant attorney general after his term as governor. From 1919 to 1933 he represented Illinois as a member of the US House of Representatives.

Richard Yates's major contributions: He stayed in the public eye after twice being defeated in runs for governor, and he courageously protected Illinois's black citizens during the race riots.

25

CHARLES SAMUEL DENEEN
1905–1913

Deneen graduated from what is today Northwestern's Law School, was an attorney for the Chicago Sanitary District, and served as the Cook County state's attorney.

As governor of Illinois, he was a strong advocate for public education and worked hard to open up streams of revenue for the public schools. He also laid the groundwork for substantial state contributions to higher education. He was truly an "education governor."

After an unsuccessful bid for a third term as governor, he was appointed to the US Senate.

Charles Deneen's major contribution: He focused on improving education in Illinois.

26

EDWARD FITZSIMMONS DUNNE
1913–1917

Edward Dunne grew up in Peoria, Illinois, and eventually attended what is known today as Northwestern University, where he obtained his law degree. He began his public life as a judge in Cook County and was a two-term mayor of Chicago.

As governor of Illinois, Dunne put much effort into public utilities and oversaw a law that allowed local municipalities to become involved with utility plants.

After Dunne lost in a bid to once again be governor, he worked as an attorney for the Cook County Board of Election Commissioners, his last public service position.

Dunne wrote extensively in retirement, publishing a series of excellent books on Illinois history.

Edward Dunne's major contributions: It may well have been his writing after having served as governor.

27

FRANK ORREN LOWDEN
1917–1921

Lowden grew up in Iowa and was a graduate of Iowa State University (Go Cyclones!). He worked as a schoolteacher to earn money to attend Union College (Northwestern University today) Law School.

After law school, he practiced law in Chicago and married a daughter of George Pullman (the ultra-wealthy railcar manufacturing tycoon, a major American industrialist).

Before being elected governor, Lowden was a member of the US House of Representatives from 1906 to 1911.

Lowden gained a national reputation after leading an intelligent reorganization of Illinois government and for his very effective handling of Chicago's 1919 race riots. His reputation was such that he was a serious contender for the Republican nomination for the presidency in 1920. He lost at a contentious convention to Warren G. Harding. Lowden was not interested in being vice president.

After his governorship, Lowden became involved in agricultural issues and led the American Farm Foundation, an institution so dear to him he bequeathed most of his estate to that organization.

Frank Lowden's major contributions: He was noted for his managerial and organizational skills and was a competent administrator.

28

LENNINGTON SMALL
1921–1929

Lennington "Len" Small was the first of Illinois's governors to come under suspicion for significant criminal wrongdoing. While serving as governor, he was indicted for operating a money-laundering scheme that took place when he had been Illinois treasurer. He was acquitted of the charges. It is interesting to note, however, that four of the jurors that acquitted Small received state jobs after the trial.

When Small was governor, he had notorious bootlegger Spike O'Donnell released from prison. O'Donnell then returned to Chicago to once again become a prominent gangster.

Len Small's major contributions: Unfortunately, his legacy was to be Illinois's first governor associated with significant wrongdoing.

29

LOUIS LINCOLN EMMERSON
1929–1933

Emmerson was a downstate businessman and banker before entering politics. His first foray into state politics was an unsuccessful bid to be state treasurer in 1912. In 1916, he became Illinois's secretary of state, a position he held for twelve years.

Emmerson became the twenty-ninth governor of Illinois on January 14, 1929, and held the office for four years. He was Illinois governor during the Great Depression.

Governor Emmerson lessened penalties for overdue taxes and issued emergency bonds to help the state grapple with the Depression. He also oversaw the first unemployment program for the state and obtained federal grants for work to be completed on the Lakes-to-the-Gulf Waterway.

Louis Emmerson's major contributions: He helped see the state through the beginnings of the Great Depression.

30

HENRY HORNER
1933–1940

Governor Horner was the states' first Jewish governor; he was a graduate of Chicago-Kent Law School (as was Emily Jansen, to whom this book is dedicated). He was a prominent Chicago lawyer. He went from eighteen years on the bench as a Cook County probate judge to the governorship.

Horner oversaw the end of Prohibition and the institution of a 2 percent state sales tax, as well as a state tax on real estate and personal property.

He became quite ill during his second term and basically conducted state business from his bed.

Horner owned one of the nation's largest collections of Lincoln memorabilia.

Henry Horner's major contributions: He made history as being the state's first Jewish governor.

31

JOHN HENRY STELLE
1940–1941

John Stelle became Illinois's thirty-first governor when Henry Horner, his predecessor, died in office. Stelle, of course, was lieutenant governor at the time.

Prior to serving as lieutenant governor, Stelle was the state's treasurer. He was very active in Democratic politics and was a delegate to the Democratic National Convention from 1928 to 1960.

John Stelle's major contributions: He was governor for only ninety-nine days, leaving little time for him to make a significant impact on the state.

32

DWIGHT HERBERT GREEN
1941–1949

Governor Green is best known for being part of the legal team that finally put Al Capone behind bars. He ran for governor on this fame and promised an anticorruption administration. When in office, he did little to combat corruption, and there has been speculation that it was campaign contributions from gangsters that allowed him to pursue the governorship.

Dwight Green's major contributions: He is really best known for his involvement in the Capone case; his administration broke the string of control of the governor's mansion by Democrats.

33

ADLAI EWING STEVENSON
1949–1953

Illinois's thirty-third governor was a man of great national and international importance and consequence. Stevenson hailed from a family with a rich tradition of public service; most famously, he was John F. Kennedy's ambassador to the United Nations. Stevenson had the unenviable task of running for president twice against the popular war hero, Dwight D. Eisenhower, losing in 1952 and 1956. He again tried to be his party's nominee for president in 1960 but lost that bid to John F. Kennedy.

Stevenson's young life was marred by a shooting accident in his home; he accidentally killed another teen. He accepted full responsibility for this and talked freely and with regret about it.

Stevenson dropped out of Harvard Law to become a journalist but resumed the study of law at Northwestern University, where he eventually earned his degree.

Despite being an Illinois governor and a two-time Democratic nominee for president, Stevenson is best known for his stint as ambassador to the United Nations. At the UN, Stevenson confronted the Soviet Union for placing nuclear weapons in Cuba. The Soviets declined to comment initially on Stevenson's accusations, which he backed up with conclusive evidence. Stevenson famously told the Soviets that he would "wait until hell freezes over" for their response. This performance made Stevenson one of the heroes of the Cold War.

Adlai Stevenson's major contributions: He was widely admired for his unrepentant liberalism, intelligence, and wit.

34

WILLIAM GRANT STRATTON
1953–1961

Stratton was a progressive Republican. He provided beds for inmates in Illinois hospitals, appointed the first woman to a high cabinet position, allowed state sales tax to be used for schools, and floated a bond issue to benefit the state tollway system.

Prior to serving as governor, he served as state treasurer and also served one term in the US House of Representatives.

Stratton tried unsuccessfully to spend a third term in the governor's mansion.

William Stratton's major contributions: His efforts for educational financing and the tollways were significant.

35

OTTO KERNER JR.
1961–1968

Palindrome? Check.

Governor? Check.

Inmate? Check.

War hero? Check.

General? Check.

Federal Judge? Check.

Kaiser? No.

Kerner had quite the academic pedigree. He was a graduate of Cambridge University as well as Northwestern University's College of Law. He served during World War II in North Africa and Europe and was a true war hero. During the war, among many acts of valor, he saved a fellow GI from drowning off the coast of Italy. Kerner left the army after World War II as a colonel and eventually obtained the rank of general while serving in the Illinois National Guard after the war.

Kerner was elected governor twice but resigned in 1968 to accept an appointment as judge on the US Court of Appeals.

Sadly, Kerner was tried and convicted for racetrack fraud and bribery. He spent time in prison but was paroled after being diagnosed with cancer.

Otto Kerner's major contributions: Without his criminal conviction, he would have been remembered as a competent governor, judge, and war hero. Sadly, he is now remembered as one of several Illinois governors that has spent time in the old "Gray Bar Hotel."

36

SAMUEL HARVEY SHAPIRO
1968–1969

Shapiro became governor for a brief period of time after Otto Kerner resigned to become a federal judge. He ran for reelection to become governor in his own right but was narrowly defeated by Richard Ogilvie.

Shapiro was an immigrant success story, having been born in Estonia.

After retiring from politics, he spent his life contributing his time and efforts to promote his old college fraternity, Alpha Epsilon Pi.

Samuel Shapiro's major contributions: Shapiro, like Kerner, was a war hero and former general. He did not serve as governor long enough to really distinguish himself.

37

RICHARD BUELL OGILVIE
1969–1973

Governor Ogilvie was an extraordinarily accomplished, respected, and competent public servant. He was widely viewed as an honest and incorruptible man.

After dropping out of Yale to volunteer for the army, Ogilvie served as a tank commander during World War II. He was wounded in this conflict.

After the war, he, like Emily Jansen years after him, attended Chicago-Kent College of Law. From 1954 to 1955, he served as US Attorney in the Chicago area, and from 1958 to 1961, he battled organized crime in the Chicago area as a special assistant to the US Attorney. In 1962, he served as Cook County sheriff and was on the Cook County Board from 1967 to 1969. After serving as president of the Cook County Board, he was elected governor.

After his stint as governor, Ogilvie remained active in public life. He was a serious candidate for the job of FBI director but was not appointed by President Nixon. In 1979, he became publisher of the resurrected *Chicago Daily News,* and in 1987, he was appointed by Secretary of Transportation Elizabeth Dole to chair a committee to explore the feasibility of defunding Amtrak, the nation's railroad system.

His last job was as a member of Isham, Lincoln, and Beale, a Chicago law firm cofounded by Abraham Lincoln's son.

Ogilvie is entombed at Rosehill Cemetery in Chicago. Richard Ogilvie's major contributions were related to his cleaning up corruption.

38

DANIEL WALKER
1973–1977

Dan Walker famously walked across the entire state of Illinois when campaigning for the governorship. He also holds the distinction of becoming a prison inmate after he served as the state's chief executive.

Walker served as an officer in the US Navy during World War II. After the war, he attended law school at Northwestern University.

Prior to becoming governor, Walker was a seasoned business executive, most notably at the now defunct Montgomery Ward department store.

Walker's first foray into the public arena was as head of a study team that reviewed police behavior during the 1968 Democratic Convention in Chicago. The team found that the police had acted unprofessionally, and that a "police riot" had occurred.

Walker narrowly defeated Richard Ogilvie, a popular and respected figure, for the governorship in 1972.

Walker was a relatively ineffectual governor. He ran as an "anti-machine" Democrat and was defeated for reelection in the primary by a candidate backed by Chicago Mayor Richard J. Daley.

In the 1980s, he started a car lube business and acquired a savings and loan association, and eventually was imprisoned due to illegalities associated with his conduct as director of the savings and loan.

As this book is being written in 2012, Daniel Walker is supporting an effort to keep Governor Pat Quinn from expanding casino gambling in the state.

39

JAMES ROBERT THOMPSON
1977–1991

Big Jim Thompson was extraordinarily popular; he was Illinois's longest-serving governor. He kept the White Sox in Chicago, put a former Illinois governor in jail, and tried his best to spring another Illinois governor out of prison. Well respected nationally, many speculated as to why he did not run for the nation's highest office.

Thompson attended the University of Illinois when its Chicago campus was in its infancy. He was also a graduate of Northwestern University Law School.

Thompson had an impressive career as a lawyer before becoming governor. He taught law for a time at Northwestern. President Nixon appointed him the US Attorney for Northern Illinois, and Thompson proceeded in prosecuting Democratic and Republican politicos, eventually convicting former Illinois Governor Otto Kerner for using improper influence for the horse-racing industry. He also convicted many of Mayor Richard J. Daley's key allies, such as Alderman Tom Kean and County Clerk Matt Danaher. Republicans did not escape his prosecutions; he also put away Republican County Commissioner Floyd Fulle.

Thompson was Illinois's first governor to garner over three million votes; he was elected four times, though he only narrowly defeated Adlai Stevenson III for governor in his third gubernatorial campaigns. (He more handily defeated Stevenson in the rematch four years later.)

In 1980, Thompson froze all state hiring and required all hires to go through a Governor's Office of Personnel. Alleged patronage abuses led to the Supreme Court ending this practice.

Thompson almost single-handedly saved the White Sox for Chicago by literally twisting arms in Springfield and developing an authority that built a stadium in Chicago for the White Sox so they would stay in the city.

After serving as governor, Thompson served on the commission that studied 9/11.

Thompson now works for a prestigious law firm in Chicago and has donated his services attempting to spring former Illinois Governor George Ryan from jail.

A large state building in Chicago is named after Jim Thompson.

James Thompson's major contributions: As a Republican, he attracted many Democratic supporters and received a good deal of support from traditionally Democratic constituencies.

40

JAMES EDGAR
1991–1999

Following a popular and larger-than-life governor like fellow Republican Jim Thompson was not easy, but Edgar succeeded in becoming as well respected as his predecessor.

Edgar, a graduate of Eastern Illinois University in Charleston, served in the Illinois House for two terms, being elected in 1976 and 1978. He was appointed Illinois's secretary of state in 1981, replacing Alan Dixon, who was appointed US senator. Edgar then went on to win two terms as Illinois's secretary of state on his own, serving in that position from 1981 to 1991.

When Edgar was governor, Republicans dominated both Illinois legislative bodies, so he was able to pursue his agenda items quite effectively. He oversaw a state surplus, downsized government, and saw to it that the state began paying its bills on time.

After serving as governor, Edgar was approached about running against Barack Obama for Illinois's open US Senate seat. He declined, citing health concerns.

Edgar's administration did experience a couple of interesting controversies. He declared an L. Ron Hubbard Day, to honor the founder of Scientology, and then rescinded his declaration. Also, a company that contributed to his campaign overcharged the state for some services. Some people were indicted for this, but Edgar was not.

James Edgar's major contributions: He achieved fiscal prudence and streamlined government. Edgar left office a popular (though not charismatic) and respected public servant.

41

GEORGE HOMER RYAN
1999–2003

George Ryan is a pharmacist from Kankakee. He served in the army during the Korean conflict.

Ryan was a state legislator from 1973 to 1983, was lieutenant governor from 1983 to 1991, and was secretary of state from 1991 to 1998.

Unfortunately, Ryan is best known for the "License for Bribes" scandal. Ryan was convicted, and is currently in prison, because, while serving as Illinois's secretary of state, driver's licenses were fraudulently given to people who had paid bribes. Unfortunately, one of the people receiving such a license was a truck driver who was later involved in a fatal auto accident.

Ryan is in jail for the actions that occurred when he served as secretary of state. The reasons he has given for getting out of prison are his age, his long government service, and the health of family members (two of whom have died during his prison term). Former Illinois Governor Jim Thompson, currently an attorney, has been trying to spring Ryan from the penitentiary.

George Ryan's major contributions: He is remembered most for the unfortunate scandal.

41

ROD BLAGOJEVICH
2003–2009

Blagojevich was Illinois's first (and so far only) governor to be impeached. He is also the state's only governor to appear on reality television shows, often doing an Elvis impersonation. "Blago," as the press called him, became a laughingstock. The people of Illinois elected this man twice. He did, however, possess the best head of hair that any Illinois governor has ever had.

Blagojevich was put away by a federal prosecutor for trying to sell Illinois's US Senate seat (which became vacant when Barack Obama was elected president). The prosecutor famously said that Lincoln would roll over in his grave if he got wind of Blago's shenanigans. Blagojevich is now serving time in federal prison in Littleton, Colorado, for this crime that led to his impeachment, arrest, and conviction.

While in office, Blago spent little time in the state's capital, preferring to work from Chicago.

Blagojevich was a Golden Gloves boxer as a youth and graduated from Pepperdine Law School, after an undergraduate career at Northwestern University in Evanston, Illinois.

Blago was a private attorney, a member of the Illinois General Assembly, a US congressman, and eventually the state's governor. As governor, he had a contentious relationship with the legislative branch and with his own lieutenant governor. Blagojevich was able to enact legislation expanding health care and was able to provide for free public transit for senior citizens, but his eccentric behavior while in office is what he will be most remembered for.

Blagojevich was really propelled into office in many ways because he married the right woman. His father-in-law was an influential Chicago alderman that was instrumental in Rod's being elected to the US House of Representatives and to the governor's mansion. Blago fought publicly with his wife's family while in office, even though he arguably owed his political career to them.

Before his criminal trial, Blago made the rounds of national television talk shows, proclaiming is innocence. He was on "Celebrity Apprentice" but his wife was on "I'm a Celebrity, Get me Out of Here"; he unsuccessfully sought to be released from travel restrictions in order to appear on "I'm a Celebrity"; his wife appeared on the show instead.

When appearing on "The David Letterman Show," he told the host that he had always wanted to be on the program in "the worst way." Letterman assured him that he was. That exchange was a perfect way to sum up Blago's sad and embarrassing career.

42

PAT QUINN
2009–Present

Pat Quinn did his undergraduate work at Georgetown University in the nation's capital and received his JD from Northwestern University's School of Law.

Quinn started his professional life working as a tax attorney and served as an aide to Governor Dan Walker. He sought to empower the people of Illinois by making voter referendums easier to accomplish, but his gathering of petitions supporting his proposed amendment to the state's constitution was ruled unconstitutional.

While attending law school, Quinn spearheaded an effort to reduce the size of the Illinois House of Representatives. This made him popular with most people, as Illinois is often viewed as being a bit top heavy government-wise, but it was pretty unpopular with the state's politicians.

In 1982, he served on the Cook County Commission of Tax Appeals. He helped create the Citizens Utility Board, an agency that acts as a watchdog over the state's various utilities.

Quinn lost a bid to be the state's treasurer in 1986 and then became an aide to Chicago Mayor Harold Washington.

He served as Illinois's treasurer from 1991 to 1995. He ran unsuccessfully for secretary of state against George Ryan. His main campaign theme in this contest was pointing out that Ryan had given vanity license plates to his friends and state officials.

He lost a bid to become lieutenant governor and then successfully won election as lieutenant governor for Rod Blagojevich, a man he admitted he rarely spoke with and had a poor relationship with.

Quinn succeeded Blago as governor when the latter was impeached, and then he earned election as governor in his own right.

Quinn's major task at the time of this writing is fixing the finances of the state, especially its unsustainable pension obligations.

Quinn succeeded a governor who is currently in jail (Blagojevich), and ran for secretary of state against another man who is now incarcerated (Ryan). When he was young, he served as an aide to Dan Walker, who also spent some time in prison.

PART TWO
The Mayors of Chicago

William Ogden (1837–1838)

Buckner Morris (1838–1839)

Benjamin Raymond (1839–1840, 1842–1843)

Alexander Loyd (1840–1841)

Francis Sherman (1841–1842, 1862–1863, 1863–1865)

Augustus Garrett (1843–1844, 1845–1846)

Alson Sherman (1844–1845)

John Chapin (1846–1847)

James Curtiss (1847–1848, 1850–1851)

James Woodworth (1848–1849)

Walter Gurnee (1851–1852)

Charles Gray (1853–1854)

Isaac Milliken (1854–1855)

Levi Boone (1855–1856)

Thomas Dyer (1856–1857)

John Wentworth (1857–1858, 1860–1861)

John Haines (1858–1860)

Julian Ramsey (1861–1862)

John Rice (1865–1869)

Roswell Mason (1869–1871)

Joseph Medill (1871–1873)

Lester Legrant Bond (1873)

Harvey Colvin (1873–1876)

Monroe Heath (1876–1879)

Carter Harrison Sr. (1879–1887, 1893)

John Roche (1887–1889)

DeWitt Cregier (1889–1891)

Hempstead Washburne (1891–1893)

George Swift (1893, 1895–1897)

John Hopkins (1893–1895)

Carter Harrison Jr. (1897–1905, 1911–1915)

Edward Dunne (1905–1907)

Fred Busse (1907–1911)

William Hale Thompson (1915–1923, 1927–1931)

William Dever (1923–1927)

Anton Cermak (1931–1933)

Frank Corr (1933)

Edward Kelly (1933–1947)

Martin Kennelly (1947–1955)

Richard Joseph Daley (1955–1976)

Michael Bilandic (1976–1979)

Jane Byrne (1979–1983)

Harold Washington (1983–1987)

Eugene Sawyer (1987–1989)

Richard Michael Daley (1989–2011)

Rahm Emanuel (2011–Present)

1

WILLIAM OGDEN
1837–1838

William Ogden is rightfully called "Chicago's Founder." He was Chicago's first mayor after its incorporation, which he helped bring about.

Ogden's father died when Ogden was young. As a teen, he took over his father's real estate business in New York. He started law school at New York University and served in the New York State Assembly before moving to Chicago.

Ogden went west to Chicago to pursue business interests and eventually became a railroad and canal businessman. He built and invested in railroads, and he lobbied the US Congress on behalf of the transcontinental railroad.

Ogden was committed to turning Chicago into a major US city. When he was mayor, if funds were not available from the city or state for improvements, he often paid for them himself.

Ogden actually designed the first swing bridge over the Chicago River; he also owned a brewery in Chicago.

Ogden was a vocal antislavery opponent but had a falling out with Abraham Lincoln and the Republican Party.

After making significant contributions as Chicago's mayor, he returned to New York.

Ogden Avenue in Chicago is named after him. There is also a street in New York City that bears his name.

2

BUCKNER MORRIS
1838–1839

Mayor Morris was a member of the Whig party. He began the practice of law in Chicago in 1834. He began serving as mayor in 1838 and served as an alderman after his mayoral term.

From 1853 to 1855, he sat as a Lake County Circuit Court judge.

Morris was adamantly opposed to the Civil War, and in 1864, he was arrested for helping Confederate prisoners of war escape Camp Douglas in Chicago. He was exonerated.

3

BENJAMIN RAYMOND
1839–1840
1842–1843

Raymond twice served as mayor of Chicago. Originally a merchant from New York State, he moved west to try his hand in the promising Chicago real estate market.

Mayor Raymond obtained the site of Fort Dearborn from the federal government for the city of Chicago and turned State Street into a wide boulevard.

After serving as mayor, Raymond was a very active and successful businessman. He built a woolen factory in Elgin, served as president of the Fox River Railroad, and provided some seed money for the Elgin Watch Company, whose first timepiece bore his name.

4

ALEXANDER LOYD
1840–1841

Loyd (his name was sometimes spelled "Lloyd") was also from New York. When he moved to Chicago, he worked as a contractor and builder. He became a volunteer firefighter and the department's head engineer. In 1835, he served on the Board of Trustees for the city of Chicago. After serving as mayor, he spent a short time as an alderman.

5

FRANCIS SHERMAN
1841–1842
1862–1863
1863–1865

Sherman, a Democrat, served three terms as mayor: 1841–1842, 1862–1863, and 1863–1865. Prior to becoming mayor, he was an alderman, Cook County commissioner, and state senator.

The *Chicago Daily American* reprinted his March 4, 1841, inaugural address, which gives some insight about him. Part of it is included here:

FELLOW CITIZENS: It having been customary for my predecessors in office to give some expression of their sentiments in entering upon their municipal duties, it would hardly be taken as an excuse, for deviating from that established custom that no portion of my life has been devoted to those studies and pursuits which qualify one for addressing the public. But in my own humble and unstudieous way, I beg leave sincerely to thank you for the great confidence you have manifested in my abilities in placing me at the head of your municipal government, and to hope that my official conduct will be such as to still further strengthen it. It would only be the reiteration of a sentiment common to all good citizens, and one which all will acknowledge, were I to say that the object nearest my heart, is the welfare of our city in all its interests. My only faults, I hope, will be those arising from inexperience and error of judgment; for I can assure you that I need but know the right to diligently pursue it.

6

AUGUSTUS GARRETT
1843–1844
1845–1846

Mayor Garrett owned a lucrative auction house in Chicago before becoming mayor. He is best known for having his second election invalidated due to fraud. As mayor, he converted a large elementary school into an insane asylum.

After his death, his wife established the Garrett Evangelical Theological Seminary in Evanston, Illinois, in his honor.

Garrett's first inaugural address, carried in the March 14, 1843, *Chicago Democrat,* gives a great deal of insight into him. Part of it is included here:

Fellow Citizens & Gentlemen of the Common Council:

Having been elected to the office I have the [approx. 6 characters illegible] to hold by an overwhelming majority of [approx. 14 characters illegible] of my fellow citizens, were I on this the earliest official occasion of meeting you; to [approx. 8 characters illegible] an expression of my feelings. I cannot [approx. 7 characters illegible] my election in any other light than as a [approx. 4 characters illegible] mark of public confidence, that through [approx.4 characters illegible] efforts, however humble, the character of our City will be sustained both at home and abroad, of public confidence also, that, as the first representative of the City in its councils, my best exertions will be used to subserve its interests, preserve its morals, and maintain law and good order throughout the community. To that party to which I more especially owe my election, I need only say, that if I shall be instrumental in carrying out, during my term of office, to any extent however small, its comprehensive first principle of the greatest good to the greatest number, I shall consider that I shall have discharged my duty to it, knowing full well that I cannot accomplish that result, but by performing conscientiously and rigidly all the duties of a faithful public servant. Happily for the party that elected me, its differences are healed, and union and harmony prevail to enable it to assert triumphantly now, and, I trust, hereafter, its elevated doctrines; but although I view my election, as the triumphant assertion of a great principle, I yet feel that no political motives nor party bias will ever tempt me to sacrifice, in any degree, the welfare of our flourishing City, but that in every thing pertaining to the public interest, I shall consult the public good and advocate measures tending to the public prosperity, unbiased by party considerations.

7

ALSON SHERMAN
1844–1845

Mayor Sherman was born in Barre, Vermont. He started Chicago's first sawmill and was the chief of the fire department before becoming mayor. Not surprisingly, he emphasized building a good fire department as mayor. His first run for mayor was invalidated due to "illegal proceedings."

After serving as mayor, he was a trustee at Northwestern University and developed a large marble quarry in south suburban Lemont, Illinois.

8

JOHN CHAPIN
1846–1847

Chapin really left his mark as a merchant, rather than as mayor of Chicago. Prior to serving as mayor, he was an alderman from Chicago's First Ward and the vice president of the Chicago Board of Trade.

9

JAMES CURTISS
1847–1848
1850–1851

Prior to coming to Chicago from the east, Curtiss worked as an editor and printer. He also spent time as a postmaster, an important position in those days. He left his postmaster's job under some suspicion.

After moving to Chicago, he became the editor of the *Chicago Democrat*, was appointed state's attorney, and had a short-lived law practice.

During the financial panic of 1837, he tried to delay the opening of Municipal Court to slow foreclosures.

Curtiss sat on Chicago's first Board of Health, was an alderman, and was active in the Chicago Temperance Society.

In 1845, he was appointed the first clerk of the Cook County Court.

Curtiss was buried in City Cemetery. When this cemetery was developed into Lincoln Park, his body was lost.

Rumor has it he voted for John F. Kennedy in 1960, many years after his death.

10

JAMES WOODWORTH
1848–1849

James Woodworth was an extremely accomplished man with a compelling life story. Woodworth was from New York. His father died when Woodworth was young, which led to Woodworth's limited formal education; he ran the family farm at age nineteen. Because his father died when he was young, he was exceptionally close to his brothers personally and in terms of his career.

Woodworth worked as a schoolteacher, briefly worked for his brother (who was a physician), and then worked as a banker.

Woodworth also helped build the Erie Canal and opened a small dry goods store in Pennsylvania.

Woodworth moved to Chicago in 1837, the first year it was officially a city. He opened a dry goods store in Chicago. He also worked on the Illinois-Michigan Canal and operated a flour mill in nearby La Salle County.

His political career was impressive. He served in the Illinois Senate from 1839 to 1842, in the Illinois House from 1842 to 1847, and as an alderman from 1845 to 1848.

As mayor, he oversaw the opening of the Illinois-Michigan Canal and worked hard to make Chicago a center of the nation's railway system. This allowed Chicago to become a major American city.

His tenure as mayor was marked by several challenges: a severe cholera outbreak, major flooding, and a large fire.

In his second term, Mayor Woodworth put the city's financial house in order.

After serving as mayor, he was a successful and influential banker and helped make Chicago a major financial city. He served a term in the US House of Representatives and was influential in the founding of the University of Chicago, one of the world's premier institutions of higher education.

Woodworth was a personal friend and backer of Abraham Lincoln, helping Lincoln behind the scenes.

After Woodworth's death, a prairie reserve was named after him. This reserve reminds Illinois residence of what the state used to look like. It is located in Glenview and is cared for and operated by the University of Illinois-Chicago.

11

WALTER GURNEE
1851–1852

Ever been to the Great America Amusement Park in Gurnee, Illinois? The town of Gurnee is named after Chicago Mayor Walter Gurnee.

Walter, like many Chicago mayors before him, lived in New York before moving to the west to find his fortune. Gurnee was the main owner of a very successful tannery and leather works in Chicago and amassed an impressive fortune.

Gurnee's major reason for running for office was to see to it that Chicago's water supply was public owned. He accomplished that goal.

Gurnee also ran for mayor in 1860 against "Long John" Wentworth but lost.

Next time you ride the Demon at Great America, think of the mayor of Chicago, who gave the public ownership of the water supply, or think about buying a corn dog. Your choice.

12

CHARLES GRAY
1853–1854

New York State supplied yet another Chicago mayor. Candlestick maker, railroader, contractor, and manufacturer, he eventually became a rather unremarkable Chicago mayor.

The *Chicago Tribune* reprinted his inaugural address in its March 8, 1853, edition. Part of it is included here:

Gentlemen of the Council and Fellow Citizens: Before taking my seat as the presiding officer at this Board, and in accordance with the usage heretofore adopted on occasions of this kind, I take this opportunity to express my thanks for the testimonial of your kind regards and confidence in electing my humble self to fill the office of Mayor of our city. I do this with the deepest sense of my want and ability to fill the office to which I have been called by the votes of my fellow citizens.

Called, as I have been by my personal friends backed by the most unequivocal intimation of a generous public, to serve you, I feel that deep sense of obligation that no language can express for the honor that the citizens of Chicago have done me; and I can only say that, with such poor ability as I possess, the citizens of Chicago may depend on my entire devotion, to promote the interest and honor of our city and the welfare of her citizens.

Gentlemen, it is with much anxiety and trepidation that I have presumed to address myself to the task of presiding over and directing the affairs of our city, but I feel encouraged, as I trust I shall have the matured and kindly counsels of this honorable board to direct and their hearty support in executing and carrying out all such measures as may be deemed of importance to the interest, dignity and honor of the city, or the welfare of her citizens.

13

ISAAC MILLIKEN
1854–1855

Milliken hailed from Maine and opened a blacksmith's shop on Randolph Street in 1837. He entered politics and became an alderman and a judge, and then he won election an as mayor as an anti-temperance candidate. After he was sworn in, he became pro-temperance. After serving as mayor, he became a magistrate.

City Council minutes reflect his inaugural address on March 15, 1854. A portion of this address is included below:

Fellow Citizens and Gentlemen of the Common Council:

By the will of the majority of the voters of our city expressed through the Ballot Box, at our late Municipal Election, I have been called to preside over your deliberations for the present municipal year.

It is with pride I am able to state that it is to the laboring classes, principally, I am indebted for the position I now occupy.

I shall enter upon the duties of my office untramelled. I have pledged myself to no party, sect, creed, or interest; except the pledge that I have just made before you, and in presence of Almighty God, to the interest of the city. It will be my ambition to redeem that pledge.

I am aware that I have taken upon myself a heavy responsibility. The unprecedented increase in the population, resources and business of our city, demands the combined wisdom and executive ability of the municipal authorities; and, Gentlemen of the Common Council, I demand and expect your confidence and support in the discharge of the arduous duties devolving upon me. It will give me pleasure, with that confidence and support to co-operate with you in whatever measures your wisdom may desire for the government of the city.

The Legislature of our State has conferred upon you the power to legislate for our city to a limited extent. That power should be used with great discretion, and every act meet with due deliberation.

Our citizens, a large portion of whom are foreigners by birth, coming from different parts of Europe, speak various languages; nevertheless, the masses are law-abiding, peaceable and industrious, cheerfully submitting to good and wholesome laws. This is obvious to any one making the contrast between our city and others of equal importance in the Union. The absence of violent outbreaks and riots is the best evidence of the attachment of the masses to our institutions.

All laws should be made for the general good, and although such laws may sometimes conflict with individual interests, a firmness on the part of the Executive officers, and the patriotism of the citizens, will always triumph over opposition, from whatever quarter.

Gentlemen you have been called upon by your constituents to discharge no ordinary duties. The well-being of our growing city depends in a great measure upon you; for not only will the acts of this Council be felt during the present, but for years to come.

It is hoped that all party and sectional animosities will be kept out of your Councils, and that there will be a united effort on your part to advance the general interests of the city.

Your early attention will be called to the peculiar state of the finances. Although the credit of the city stands fair, and its general resources are ample, yet the immediate demands upon the Treasury, and the limited available resources to meet those demands, require great skill and economy in that department. The late Council has anticipated largely the resources of the city for the present year. The Charter limits the Council to the use of the credit of the city to the extent of one hundred thousand dollars in any one year.

14

LEVI BOONE
1855–1856

Who would want to run against a relative of Daniel Boone? Levi was his grandnephew. It would be like running against a relative of Oprah's in the Chicago of our times.

Boone was a very divisive, nativist governor. He was a member of the "Know-Nothing Party" (How could a party stand for a name like that?).

Boone made sure only people born on American soil could work for the city. Further, he outlawed beer and liquor sales on Sunday, which really alienated German American Chicagoans.

His inaugural address was carried in the *Daily Democrat* on March 14, 1855. Part of it is recounted below:

Gentlemen of the Common Council: Having been, by the partiality of my fellow citizens, elevated to the honorable and responsible position of Mayor of this city, the future metropolis of the West, it becomes my duty, in compliance with universal custom, to present to you my views, in relation to the policy and principles by which we should be governed by our administration.

First, however, indulge me gentlemen, in an expression of the gratitude which I feel, for so flattering a token of the favor of my fellow citizens towards me, and their confidence in my humble abilities to serve them in this high position: a result the more grateful to me from the fact that it has been voluntary on the part of my fellow citizens, without even an announcement by me or by my authority, of my name as a candidate for that office; and still more so, from the fact that it was secured without any of those demoralizing and disgraceful appliances and influences so generally resorted to in political contests.

I am before you, gentlemen of the Common Council, untrammelled by embarrassing pledges to any individual, free to pursue just such a course of policy as my sense of duty and the best interests of our city may dictate; and with your co-operation, that liberty and that conviction of duty shall be, to the utmost of my ability, consecrated with singleness of purpose, to the greatest good of our constituents and our city.

Allow me in general terms to say, that my desire is that the strictest economy may be exercised in the expenditure of the public treasure, that no funds should be drawn from the treasury for trifling and unimportant objects, nor for purposes not clearly contemplated and authorized by the City Charter. By this I do not simply mean the purchase of "silver headed canes," or "Aldermanic Suppers;" these are unimportant, except as they may be regarded and referred to, as precedents for much more magnificent abuses. In this connection I would recommend the passage of an ordinance, providing that no moneys be drawn from the City Treasury until ordered by a vote of the Common Council, as I am persuaded that the practice which has heretofore prevailed is liable to great abuses. And for the purpose of a greater security against the allowance of improper claims, I would advise the creation of an additional Standing Committee, to be called the "Auditing Committee," whose duty it shall be carefully to examine all bills referred to it before they are acted upon by the Council.

15

THOMAS DYER
1856–1857

Dyer was originally from Connecticut. Son of a Revolutionary War officer, he served one term in the Illinois legislature and was a two-time delegate to the Democratic National Convention. He was also a successful businessman in the packing and transporting of grain. Prior to becoming mayor, he was the president of the Chicago Chamber of Commerce.

The following was the inaugural address of Mayor Dyer:

In assuming the duties of Mayor of Chicago, custom as well as propriety has made it necessary that the person chosen to that office should present some general remarks, indicating the course of policy marked out by himself for the administration of municipal affairs during his term of office. In performing this duty, fellow citizens, my remarks shall be brief. To enter into details cannot be expected, and I shall leave them to time, which develops all things. Nor is it required that in general observations I should extend my remarks, because it is well known that I was nominated as a candidate for Mayor as a member of a political party; that I was supported and opposed as the nominee of that party against the combination of all other parties, and while I am free to declare, that in all that pertains to the welfare and prosperity of our magnificent city, I shall conduct my office with no view other than that of the general weal and common benefit of all citizens of all parties, candor compels me to declare freely and fully, that my political course, my public policy, my patronage and power shall be devoted to and shaped so as to render Chicago the beneficiary of a successful application to her wants and necessities, of the great cardinal and conservative principles of the National

Democratic party. I shall be Mayor of Chicago—of all Chicago—knowing no distinction of party or sect; but I should be false to the friends who elected me, were I to forget for one moment that I am a Democrat, and that I owe my election to the confidence reposed in my fidelity to the political principles of my party.

It is not likely that political friends or political opponents will forget, that in the recent election, party politics were made the issue upon which turned the choice of officers. My opponent was my personal friend, and nothing, I suppose, but the very wide difference in our political sentiments, could have placed us in a position of antagonism. I was the candidate of one political party; against the long established and well known principles of that party were arrayed all the hostile parties and fragments of parties, which, it was supposed, when united, held a large political preponderance in this city. Every issue that could be supposed would draw from me even a single vote, was boldly presented and urged. Renegade Democrats, and men personably respectable and individually estimable, but whose political opinions had received their last modification, while writhing under the mortification of failing to receive office from our party, came forth from the oblivion into which they had shrunk, and at public meetings talked flippantly of "digging out," and stooping to reach Democrats. They lent their names to "calls," and to public meetings, invoking the people not to allow a triumph to that party from which they had withdrawn when they discovered that public offices could be filled without requiring their services. Men rejected by the Democratic party as applicants for office, are the natural allies of those who fuse in order to obtain the handling of the public money. The victory of the 4th of March is the most expressive response that could be made to their ill-mannered, ill-tempered and ridiculous appeals. Not only was every anti-Democratic element combined against us, and every feature and principle of the Democratic creed, which might be supposed to be unpopular, presented; not only were all the deeds of violence attributed to persons in Kansas brought to bear upon us, but all the political and personal sins of every individual belonging to our party in Chicago, were heaped upon our backs. I was a Know Nothing one day, and the next was said to have been black-balled. I was represented as the candidate of the saloons on the one hand, and as having voted for prohibition and the quart law on the other. I was accused of being a Douglas man, and a Democrat approving the Nebraska act, and as this was almost the only accusation made against me that was true, it was the only one that I never denied. I refer to these things in order to remind you upon what political grounds I was chosen Mayor, and that it may be known that in the discharge of my duties, I intend to maintain inviolate the principles involved in the contest just terminated.

In regard to that branch of my duties, the appointing power, I wish it to be distinctly understood, that I intend to appoint no man to office who is not, in my opinion, fitted for the place. While I shall have due regard for political friends, I intend, so far as I can, to demonstrate that good, and faithful and competent officers can be obtained, even when political associates are preferred. While I shall make no difference against naturalized citizens on account of their birth, I shall equally respect the native citizen. Birth place shall not influence me for or against applicants for office. It is needless for me, perhaps, to say that I entertain no sentiment or feeling in sympathy with those who would make birth place or creed a test for office, or for the exercise of political right.

Fellow citizens, the grand geographical position of Chicago has long since marked her out as the metropolis of the Mississippi Valley. Her name and her fame is as wide-spread as the commerce of the Union. Grain from Chicago finds its way to every port open to American vessels. Against her growing wealth, her extending prosperity and commercial greatness, rival cities and rival States attempt to raise obstacles and impediments calculated to deter settlement here. One of the most dangerous of these representations against Chicago, is that it is naturally unhealthy, and that she must be scourged annually by some prevailing epidemic. That this has prevailed to some extent to our injury, is quite probable; and the fact that the cholera has visited us one or two seasons has afforded some show of justification for the allegation of unhealthiness in our city. It will, I trust, be the pleasure of the Common Council, to unite with me in taking early steps to do whatever may be in our power, not only to preserve the general health of Chicago, but also to prevent the introduction here of disease in any of its alarming forms. Much can be done to prevent the introduction of those alarming epidemics which have carried off so many of our population in other seasons, and the name of which carries terror to the hearts of all. In everything tending to this end, the City Council shall have my earnest and hearty co-operation. Intimately connected with the preservation of the health of the city, is the subject of a proper and efficacious system of sewerage. A plan of sewerage has lately been accepted by the City Government, and steps have been taken to put it into operation. That the plan of sewerage which has been adopted will be carried out without change or modification before it is completed, is not expected, I suppose, by any one. No work of such magnitude could be planned in a manner which the experience gained in putting it into operation would not modify and change to a very great extent. That this plan will meet, in some of its practical details, obstacles and impossibilities not easily forseen,[sic] is beyond a doubt. It is even possible that it may fail altogether. The City of Chicago will, I have no doubt, cheerfully contribute any fair sum to secure the great blessing of a good system of sewerage; yet it becomes the Government of the City, those whose especial duty it is to guard her interests and protect her treasury, to see that no extravagant expenditures be made, and no great burden of taxation imposed, until practical results will have demonstrated that a wise and beneficial and effective system has been devised and put into operation. I wish not to be understood as professing a want of faith in the wisdom or efficacy of the plan of sewerage adopted by our predecessors. I am not sufficiently acquainted with that plan to be able to express an opinion upon it. I only wish to say, that out of regard to the public interest we shall not rush heedlessly into expenditures upon what must to a great extent be mere experiment. When that experiment shall give practical proof of its value, then we will only be consulting the public good by giving it a liberal and a profitable support. Before making any further large appropriations for this work, I would earnestly recommend as a matter of strict economy, that the subject be thoroughly examined and tested, and for that purpose that the best scientific talent that can be procured in the Union, be employed. This work will cost a very large amount of money, and before embarking upon it we should, at least, have the assurance that if it fail, the very wisest and most experienced, have with us been disappointed in the result.

It is my intention to endeavor to awaken a greater interest in the City Government, and also among all our citizens, real estate owners particularly, to the necessity which exists, and the justice which demands, a more liberal policy than has been pursued towards the great marine interests of Chicago. The greatest obstruction to our marine commerce, and to the whole navigating interest which seeks a market at Chicago, is the ever badly conditioned entrance to our harbor. It is a work which has and ever will require an annual outlay to keep it even in tolerable order. I think it would be a wise economy to have that entrance at once put in a condition suitable to the wants of our city and its rapidly increasing trade. While I am one of those who think that the General Government has expended during many years on harbor improvements, large amounts at points not having a tithe of the national importance or commercial trade of Chicago; and while I am one of those who would now ask of Congress an appropriation to put our harbor in a proper condition, still, I am one of those who know the fact, that the General Government will turn a deaf ear to our wants and our application, and know also that in the meantime, our harbor is daily becoming worse, and our commercial marine, experiencing disaster after disaster, within gunshot of our houses.

Under these circumstances, the City of Chicago must submit to one of three alternatives: She must stand idly by and see her vessels wrecked, or lying off unable to enter our port; or she must leave to shippers and ship owners the heavy burden of cutting a passage for their vessels to our wharves; or she must, with that liberal spirit which would foster all pursuits and callings which pour into her lap the wealth of the North-west, take upon herself the duty of opening her harbor, and keeping it open at her own expense. She is willing to incur a heavy expense, and to impose a heavy tax upon all real estate, and the personal property of her citizens, to secure a good system of sewerage. She is willing to erect hospitals, and keep them in operation at the general expense; for the general welfare. She deals liberally at the general expense for the Fire Department. These are all highly meritorious objects, and the public yield a willing support to them. Real Estate is the grand object of property in Chicago: for all things that render that valuable, that gives it a value unequalled in the annals of any other city, real estate ought to yield a most liberal allowance. The marine commerce of Chicago, has kept even pace with the railroads. Our shippers by vessels have not decreased in number because of the establishment of railroads. The lake commerce of Chicago, and that commerce by way of the canal, which is fed by the trade on the lakes, has kept even with all the other elements of Chicago's prosperity. It has brought wealth to Chicago. It daily pours into our river its countless tons of freight. Its value to the real estate of Chicago is more than equal to that of our railroads, for the value of our railroads is considerably enhanced by the advantages they enjoy in a connection with the navigation of the lakes. I invoke then, from the real estate of Chicago, a small annual tax in behalf of the navigation interests which are obstructed at the mouth of our harbor. If the General Government will not aid us; those engaged in shipping, cannot, and ought not to be made to bear the whole burden of keeping that harbor open; and will not Chicago extend her liberal fostering care—to this important interest, and contribute to its relief. I will therefore do what is in my power, and I ask a support from the Council to appropriate a reasonable sum at an early day, to aid in opening and keeping open the entrance to our river. The amount necessary for that object will not be a large one, but if applied promptly, and if kept up regularly every season, will do much to augment the business of our shippers, and lessen the burdens they now labor under. The tax necessary to raise the amount required, will be so inconsiderable upon each property holder, that I feel sure no citizen having the welfare of the city at heart, will object to it for a moment.

It is unnecessary for me to refer to the wonderful effects produced upon our city, her trade, her commerce, her real estate, her capital and her population by the introduction of those great highways of fortune-railroads. No city in the Union has been more benefitted by the introduction of railroads than Chicago; no city in the Union has been so fortunate in having so many successful and profitable roads centering in her bounds. But still more remarkable, no city in the Union has been able to secure one-tenth of our railroad facilities without the outlay of large sums in subscription to stock, or loans of her credit. Chicago, as a city, has not invested one dollar in railroads. She stands at present, the recipient of all their immense trade, wealth and business, and yet does not hold one dollar's worth of stock in them. They have been built without her aid, and in building themselves, they have spread wide and firm the foundations of our prosperity. Inasmuch, as these railroads have made no demands upon the city as a condition precedent to their establishment here, and as they have made Chicago the grand centre of the trade and commerce of the North-west and the Mississippi Valley, as they have voluntarily come hither and made this the starting point of that other great national highway, which is to connect us with our brethren over and beyond the Rocky Mountains, and upon the shores of the Pacific; I think the city which owes so much to railroads, should deal with them with a generous-indeed, a most liberal hand. I am not nor have I ever been a friend of large corporations. In common with my Democratic brethren, I have always regarded large corporations with no very friendly feelings, yet, I think that Chicago, so far as it can be done with a strict regard for private interests and public convenience, should extend to these railroads all those facilities which the enlargement and extension of their business may require. I would treat them with a generous confidence. While I would interpose the shield of the city between the rights of a citizen and either of these corporations, I would extend to them all such facilities that can be extended to them without any loss or injury to any private individual. There is no higher duty in government than to carefully protect the citizen against itself, and against any combination or corporation having wealth and power at its command. Hence in all communities, and among all classes of society, distrust and dread of the overshadowing influence of corporations has been universally felt. It is a natural feeling, and in no breast has it been stronger than in my own. I can never surrender it. I respect it in others, and I do it so much the more readily, because I have seen the power of such corporations, wielded to the wrong and injury of private individuals, and interests and rights which had no other defence than their native justice. That corporations have no souls, has become a proverb. Still I would encourage all such corporations as our railroads, in all that enables them to add wealth to our city, to increase the value of our taxable property, and give facility to the extension of our trade and commerce. I would deal with them as I would with all others, never yield to them the right and power to injure the rights of a private citizen in any manner; but beyond that, I would treat them as I would any citizen engaged in any branch of industry tending to expand our business.

It shall be my endeavor to so conduct the affairs of Chicago, that every possible aid shall be given to the support and encouragement of the common schools. The public schools of the United States are proud monuments of the liberality of our people. They are free to all, and yet supported by the voluntary taxation of the people. I trust that the jealous care which has hitherto marked our protection of the public schools will continue unabated. Let us protect them, foster them, enlarge them, multiply them, until the city of Chicago can boast, that while her population is increasing at an unexampled rate, her free schools have increased at a corresponding rate. To know that there was school accommodation in this city furnished at the public cost, for every child in the city, would be a nobler monument to our beloved city than the stateliest edifice that in other lands yet exists to point out where pomp and grandeur once ruled, and have passed away.

Chicago has just reason to be proud of her Fire Department. Who, that has ever attended a fire in this city, even at mid-winter, that has not witnessed scenes of persevering labor, undaunted courage, skill, activity, energy and all those characteristics of men risking health, and even life, to save and protect the property of their fellow citizens. Conscious that money expended in making that department as complete as possible, in furnishing it with apparatus and all the other requisites of a thorough establishment, would be but true economy, and would lessen the hardships of the gallant men who voluntarily render their services to the public good; I shall be prepared, on all occasions, to approve and sanction the most liberal legislation in behalf of the Fire Department. In this, I shall ask and expect, a willing co-operaton on the part of the Board of Aldermen.

There is one other branch of voluntary organization for the public protection, which, so far as the city government can do so, I would be rejoiced to encourage. I refer to our volunteer military companies. Chicago has citizen soldiery of which she may well feel proud. These organizations are expensive to the individuals comprising them, and yet their main object is to have in readiness an effective arm to be used only as the last resort by the government, in maintaining law and order, and preserving the property and lives of our citizens. While I trust that we may never see the day, that the law will require the aid of a bayonet to enforce the public will, I cannot but feel that the very fact that there is a large organization of citizen soldiers ready at any moment to support the constituted authorities, must act as a preventive of violence on the one hand, and is a sure guaranty to all, that the laws must be executed. I shall be in favor of dealing liberally to this branch of our protective force.

One great source of annoyance and vexation to our citizens, has been the uncertain policy with respect to rates of license. While I intend to recall none of the evils of the past, I think we can remember them with profit. I am in favor of the establishment of a good and effective ordinance respecting the sale of liquor. In framing it, I would so provide, that while excesses should be prevented on the one hand, there shall be no proscription nor prohibition on the other. I will therefore, at an early day, invite the City Council to unite with me in fixing the rate of license at a just and reasonable rate—a rate affording the city a proper revenue, and yet not too high to afford any excuse for its non-payment. This rate, I trust, shall be established permanently, and at once, and that then the subject will be dismissed for the balance of the year.

Licenses for the sale of liquors will not be the only ones requiring our attention. Those issued to persons running vehicles for hire, are surrounded with difficulties and vexatious provisions, which I hope soon to see erased from the Statute Book. Much of the oppression connected with this class of licenses, are the many and onerous fees allowed to city officers. I am in favor of a general abolition of all such fees, commencing, if you please, with those allowed to the Mayor. I am in favor of fixing specific salaries for all offices, and the abolition of all fees. In this way all men may know the fixed rate of each license, and not be compelled to seek it by an examination of the fee bills of two or three officials.

The Police Department will be examined, and active steps taken to remove all license for abuse.

The grade of the city called the high grade, which is now in full force in this city, meets my cordial approval. I hope within the present official year to see it extended with as much despatch as possible, avoiding however, any unnecessary injury to any individual. Intimately connected with the subject of the high grade, is that of paving. Of all these matters, however, I shall have occasion hereafter to communicate with the Council more in detail.

In conclusion, fellow citizens, I shall endeavor to administer the city government upon principles of strict economy. It shall be my endeavor to deal liberally in all our undertakings, and to pay a fair price for all work performed for the city. But in awarding contracts, and making improvements, favoritism, I trust, shall be utterly excluded. I think there is wide room for economy in the support of our municipal government, and so far as that economy can be practised, I shall do it.

In all things pertaining to my duty as Mayor of Chicago, I shall endeavor, to the best of my judgment, to so conduct myself, that the whole city shall be benefitted, and wishing that in this determination I may have the support of my fellow citizens; I now proceed to the business of the office to which I have been chosen.

16

JOHN WENTWORTH
1857–1858
1860–1861

This Republican mayor was called "Long John" because he was six foot, six inches in height. He was the first of Chicago's "strong" mayors. He was the prototype.

Originally from New Hampshire, he was a printer, editor, lawyer, and eventually the editor of the *Chicago Democrat*, as well as a prominent Chicago attorney. He served five terms in the US Congress as a Democrat; after serving as mayor, he then served one term again in Washington, DC, this time as a Republican.

Long John once introduced some friends to the visiting Prince of Wales by saying, "Boys, this is the prince. Prince, these are the boys."

Wentworth cracked down on vice, especially prostitution.

After serving as mayor, he became an authority on Chicago history.

Wentworth Avenue is named after him.

17

JOHN HAINES
1858–1860

Haines had considerable public experience. He was a Chicago water commissioner, two-time state senator in Springfield, a City Council member for six years, and a two-term mayor of Chicago.

He was often called "Dusty Miller" because he owned the Chicago Flour Mills.

After serving as mayor, he had a successful career as a banker.

The City Council minutes of March 16, 1859, recount his second inaugural address, a portion of which is included here:

GENTLEMEN OF THE COMMON COUNCIL: Another year has elapsed since it became my duty to address to you the customary inaugural of the Chief Magistrate of our City. Before proceeding to enter upon the topics to which I desire to call your attention, it seems fitting that we should offer up the tribute of our thanks to the All-Wise Ruler of the Universe for his mercies to us during the past twelve months, the chiefest among which are the remarkably good health which has prevailed in our city, and the fact that, in a time of severe monetary pressure, the poorer classes—those dependent altogether upon daily labor for their support—have experienced much less suffering and destitution than during former seasons. There have been, it is true, drawbacks to our prosperity, among which are short crops in this and neighboring States, and those financial difficulties common to the whole country, if not to the civilized world. Yet these may also be, and no doubt are, designed for our ultimate benefit. A continued prosperous condition of affairs, in the end, would prove as terribly disastrous as the contrary: while an occasional check to the upward movement of trade and commerce, no doubt acts as a wholesome restraint upon speculation, and a regulator to the great industrial and commercial interests of the country. These monetary difficulties are a valuable lesson to us, also. They admonish us to retrenchment and economy in our municipal affairs, and warn us, however prosperous we may be financially, however great our ability to assume obligations at any one period, a day of reckoning is sure to come, for which we must be prepared or suffer the consequences of our folly.

I cannot also let the present occasion pass without thanking my fellow citizens for the flattering manner in which they have expressed their confidence in me and in my ability to serve them faithfully by a re-nomination and re-election to the place I now hold, accomplished, as they were, in the face of strong opposition, and which opposition was only overcome by the ardor and determination of the masses of the Republican party. Such being the circumstances accompanying my re-nomination and re-election, I feel doubly grateful to my fellow citizens, and trust that, with God helping, I shall be found worthy of the trust and confidence reposed in me.

The aspect and condition of our national affairs also call for at least a passing notice. I regret to be compelled to say that they are anything but flattering to our pride as a nation. Bribery and corruption of the worst descriptions appear to have taken deep root in the Federal Capital; while the entire energies of the general Government, its purse, its sword, and even its tribunals of justice, seem to be devoted to one sole object, and that, the spread of human slavery. Every aspirant for office is tried according to his faith upon this question, and reward or punishment meted out accordingly. Is it to be wondered at then, that in reference to our national affairs, the country teems with accounts of frauds, embezzlements of the public moneys, squanderings of the revenue and other crimes and misdemeanors? With the existence of such a condition of our federal relations but few measures for the common good can be accomplished; while those of an individual and special character, or for the benefit of particular sections have precedence. Thus the Homestead Bill, almost the only one before Congress for the benefit of the masses of the people, designed to rescue the remaining portion of our public domain from the hands of speculators, and set it apart wholly for the benefit of the people, has been defeated by pro slavery sectionalism. In my former address to you, I called attention to the beneficence of this great measure, especially in its effects upon the poor in our large cities, and I need not now enlarge upon it. A pro-slavery sectional vote also came very near depriving the masses of that great boon of modern legislation—cheap postage. I regret to say, I see no prospect of an end to these assaults upon the rights, liberties ad interests of the masses, as long as our Federal Government is under the control of a party which legislates wholly for the benefit of a class, and is deadly hostile to any measure having for its end and aim the good of the people generally, and the conservation and elevation of the free labor of the country.

18

JULIAN RAMSEY
1861–1862

A Republican, originally from New York, Ramsey made his mark as a grain dealer in Chicago, which was a national center of grain and transportation.

He served as the Cook County treasurer and was president of the Chicago Board of Trade before becoming mayor.

His inaugural address of May 6, 1861, as it appeared in the City Council minutes, gives insight into his challenges and priorities. A portion of it is included below:

Gentlemen of the Common Council: I find myself, for the first time in my life, politically, in an official position. I have been, as it were, whirled from the comparatively quiet commercial pursuits in which I have been engaged from my boyhood, into the chair of the Chief Executive of this great city of the North-West. The honor—(and truly a great honor I feel it to be)—was entirely unsought and undeserved; but the feeling that the wish of the people should command the services of every good citizen, more particularly in times like these, is the cause of my presence here to-day, in this chamber. I have never entertained the idea of occupying this or any other political place, and I appear before you now, confessing with regret, that I am but poorly qualified to perform the duties that are before me; but I am ready to do my best, and if you assist me to that end, as I have no doubt you will, there is but little doubt but all will be well. During the brief period which has elapsed, since I have been aware I was to occupy this place, I have been most of the time engaged in performing duties, which I considered paramount to any, for the good of our country, and which duties I may truly say were more congenial to my feelings, than those I now assume. I have been assisting to arm, equip, and supply our volunteers, that they might "be enabled to hold, possess, and occupy" the most important military point in our State, or indeed in the whole Valley of the Mississippi. I have, however, endeavored to obtain such information in relation to the affairs of our city, as would be useful to me in the performance of my duties, and I regret to have to state that they are not in so good condition as I could wish.

19

JOHN RICE
1865–1869

John Rice was a shoemaker known for singing in his shop. He sang his way to a career as an actor, stage manager, and theater manager in the Chicago theater scene. He brought the first opera to Chicago. Famously, when his theater caught fire, he told the patrons that he would not allow a fire in his theater. It burned anyway.

After serving as mayor, he served one partial term in the US Congress.

20

ROSWELL MASON
1869–1871

Mason came to office at a time when people thought that a businessman would do a better job of running the government than politicians. A civil engineer who built the important Illinois Central Railroad, he was elected to reform government and better manage it. He was not able to do much due to the Great Chicago Fire.

He closed taverns for a week after the fire and encouraged people to pray. Needless to say, he was not reelected.

If you want to see where the Great Chicago Fire started, go to Manny's Deli on Jefferson near Roosevelt. Next to Manny's is the Chicago Fire Academy, built on the spot the great fire started. Manny's corn beef is very good. Their matzo ball soup is to die for.

21

JOSEPH MEDILL
1871–1873

Medill was elected to rebuild Chicago after the fire. He agreed to serve only if the state legislature rewrote the Chicago City Charter to allow for a powerful mayor. It did.

Previously a lawyer and newspaper publisher (and owner of the *Chicago Tribune*), Medill was able to get state grants, federal grants, and foreign donations to rebuild the nation's fourth largest city. He changed building codes and did a competent job in helping the city make a comeback.

22

LESTER LEGRANT BOND
1873

Bond was appointed to be acting mayor when Medill took a trip to Europe. He served only one year and tried to win election on his own but failed, probably because he promised to ban Sunday liquor sales.

Prior to being mayor, Bond was a Chicago alderman from 1862 to 1864 and a member of the Illinois General Assembly from 1886 to 1870. He was one of the founding members of the Illinois Republican Party.

Politicians, especially in Illinois, must learn that banning liquor sales does not lend itself to a long political career.

23

HARVEY COLVIN
1873–1876

Colvin served as city treasurer before becoming mayor. In office just a month, he was faced with a huge mob demanding jobs and assistance. Colvin was saved by an alderman that promised food on credit to the mob to get them through the winter. Colvin repealed the ban on Sunday liquor sales.

Election laws changed, and Colvin refused to vacate his office to the incoming mayor. So for a while, Chicago actually had two mayors.

A state judge finally resolved the standoff, and Colvin was out of a job.

24

MONROE HEATH
1876–1879

The Chicago City Charter was changed in 1875, giving the mayor a longer term and more powers. Therefore, Heath served a short term and a long term.

As mayor, he saw federal troops break a railroad workers' strike in Chicago.

His inaugural address of July 24, 1876, was recounted in the City Council minutes. A part of it is highlighted here:

To the Honorable Common Council of the City of Chicago: The financial condition of the city of Chicago, in all its details and aspects, has been so thoroughly investigated and discussed, both by this Council, the public and the press of the city, that I consider it unnecessary to again enter into these details with you; but, in assuming the position of the Mayor of the city, it may not the improper that I should address to you in a general way a few words in relation to the matters which so deeply concern the welfare of this community. I know well the great interest that is felt by all classes in our municipal affairs, and that they are looking forward with hope to a speedy adjustment of all the complications which have arisen from our present financial embarrassment. I know well, also, that the trusts imposed upon me and upon you to execute are very complicated and difficult, and I enter upon the discharge of my duties with great diffidence, but with the single aim and purpose of devoting myself to the direct duties of the office, and I shall in that capacity know no party, nationality or class. In the short time I shall occupy this position it will be my earnest endeavor to act impartially, and, with your aid and assistance, to do what I can to restore this city to a sound financial condition, and to that end I ask the aid and assistance of all men who have the welfare of this city at heart to come forward and contribute their influence and their means toward maintaining the public credit and upholding the honor of this city.

25

CARTER HARRISON SR.
1879–1887
1893

Harrison was the first Chicago mayor elected five times (his son Carter Jr. was also elected five times). In 1893, a disgruntled office seeker assassinated Harrison, prompting the cancellation of the closing ceremonies of the World Columbia Exposition.

Harrison was a lawyer, US congressman, Cook County commissioner, and then a five-term mayor of Chicago. After serving as mayor, he owned a major newspaper.

During the Haymarket labor riots in 1886, he urged the police to leave the protesters alone.

In 1890 he took a trip to Yellowstone and Alaska with his daughter, turning that experience into a best-selling book.

Harrison's initial inaugural address appears in the City Council minutes of April 28, 1879. A portion of it is herein included:

Gentlemen of the Common Council— The welfare of nearly 500,000 people depends, to a large extent, upon the manner in which you may, during the next twelve months, discharge your official duties. A city sprung into existence within your own memory, but already the third in America in population, and in commercial importance ranking among the ten leading cities of the world, will have its growth and progress more or less advanced or retarded by your action. Its citizens have, within the past eight years, struggled under difficulties sufficient to paralyze any other people. Those difficulties with them have only called forth unexampled energies. They know not how to despair.

To manage the affairs of such a community is worthy of a proud ambition, and should beget in its representatives a sense of deep and earnest responsibility.

Rising from the ashes of two conflagrations unequaled in the past, Chicago and her people, burdened by an enormous debt, were at once confronted by

A FINANCIAL REVULSION, which has disturbed the social foundations of nations, Labor has struggled for bread, and has often been forced to go without sufficient food. Real estate, the foundation of wealth, which furnishes four-fifths of the city's revenues, has been laid under a heavy load of taxation. Rents being low, and sales practically impossible, land has been unable to meet its obligations. Taxation locks up money in the hands of the money dealer, where it escapes the eye of the collector, thus forcing legitimate enterprise to bear an unequal burden. This stifles energy; deters investment, and will, unless checked, dry up the sources of revenue. Chicago expects you to give her relief. She will forgive honest mistakes, but she demands of you worthy and earnest diligence.

26

JOHN ROCHE
1887–1889

Roche, a Republican, hailed from New York. Prior to becoming mayor, he was a machinery dealer. As mayor, he worked to suppress gambling in Chicago saloons. After serving as mayor, he managed the Otis Elevator Company.

His inaugural address of April 18, 1887, gives some insights into his priorities and challenges. A portion of it can be found below:

Gentlemen of the City Council: You are the chosen guardians of, and legislators for a city of 800,000 people, whose material and moral well being, and prosperity are, in large measure, committed to your care. How immense is your responsibility: How commanding the call for the right exercise of your highest faculties: And how great the reward for the faithful discharge of your duties:

To-day, Chicago is the chief distributing point of the North-West; the greatest railway center on this Continent—a living tide of over three hundred thousand souls rushing through her railway arteries daily, while the books of the Collector of Customs show a greater number of arrivals and departures of vessels from our harbor during the season of navigation, than from the port of New York.

Chicago is peopled by diverse nationalities, with different original modes of training and habits of thought and life, attracted here by the larger opportunities afforded for providing homes for themselves and their children and for laying the foundations of a prosperous future. The atmosphere of Freedom changes an exotic feature here, obliterates or smooths down a foreign wrinkle there, and contact and association assimilate their habits to those who are "to the manner born," till, in the powerful alembic of free institutions, race distinctions, prejudices and hates dissolve and disappear, and the plastic hand of Liberty moulds all nationalities into the perfect likeness of American citizenship—the grandest type of manhood the world has ever seen. Thus without violent change, or sudden shock to race or religious opinions, the equal rights of all citizens of whatever birth or creed being preserved intact, the old civilization gives place to the new, combining the patient industry, frugal habits and sturdy grip of the Old World with the quick perceptions, and elastic and expansive enterprise of the New, and forming a cosmopolitan city, whose genius is creative, not destructive. Her inspiration is to build up, not to tear down; and they most truly represent and honor her character who do most to "lengthen her cords and strengthen her stakes," and help to make Chicago the most economical, the most comfortable, and the most desirable dwelling place on this continent.

27

DEWITT CREGIER
1889–1891

Cregier holds the US patents for both the fire hydrant and the water fountain. Before serving as mayor, he worked as an engineer.

Under Cregier, the city annexed several suburbs, increasing its size significantly. Chicago also won the bid to host the World's Fair during his administration.

His inaugural address of April 15, 1889, is found in the City Council minutes. A representative segment of this address follows:

GENTLEMEN OF THE CITY COUNCIL: On the second day of May, 1837, Chicago became a city and its first municipal officers were installed. The portrait of its first mayor graces the walls of this chamber. At the first city election, according to the record, there were only six wards, having in the aggregate a population of about 4,000. The total vote cast for officers was 709; the south division contributing 408; the north division 204, and the west division 97. To the Chicagoan of to day these statistics give force to the truth of the adage: "From little acorns great oaks grow." Since the municipal acorn was planted, fifty-two years have passed and notwithstanding the vicissitudes of financial panics, desolation by flood and fire, notwithstanding discouraging obstacles incident to the march of time, the acorn planted half a century ago, nurtured by men of indomitable energy, devotion and confidence in Chicago has developed into a grand and enduring oak, spreading its majestic branches over a metropolis containing more than 850,000 people—a growth and development without a parallel in the history of the world.

As late as 1852, there were no public improvements of note, no general water supply, no system of drainage, but few paved streets, beyond plank, and comparatively few other public works. Since that date however, the march of improvement has kept pace with the demand of the great and growing metropolis of the west, as demonstrated by the character and magnitude of the public improvements in our city at the close of last year. There were then in use nearly 700 miles of water pipes, ten miles of water tunnels, 500 miles of sewers, 350 miles of paved streets, 1,000 miles of sidewalks, 25,000 street lamps, ninety-eight school buildings, twenty-one police stations, forty-nine fire department stations, seventy-six fire apparatus, thirty-six swing-bridges, thirty-three viaducts, 900 miles of city telegraph wire, a public library containing 44,000 volumes, together with the City Hall and numerous other public buildings. The bonded debt of the city is a little over $12,500,000., the water debt less than $4,000,000., and the sewer debt about $2,500,000., making a total indebtness of about 19,000,000. dollars.

28

HEMPSTEAD WASHBURNE
1891–1893

Mayor Washburne came from high political pedigree. His father was a US congressman, the nation's secretary of state, and a minister to France.

Washburne graduated from the School of Law at Northwestern University. (Prior to that, he studied metaphysics at the University of Bonn in Germany.) Before serving as mayor he was a practicing attorney, worked in the superior court, and was elected city attorney in 1885.

29

GEORGE SWIFT
1893 (Acting Mayor)
1895–1897 (Elected Mayor)

George Swift was a graduate of the University of Chicago. Before entering politics, he worked as a drug clerk and in manufacturing.

His first office as a politician was that of alderman from the Eleventh Ward. In 1885, President Chester Arthur appointed him a special agent of the US Treasury. In 1887, he was a commissioner of public works in Chicago.

As mayor of Chicago, he commissioned several of the city's large parks.

After serving as mayor, he was a successful contractor and served as president of two major Chicago area companies.

30

JOHN HOPKINS
1893–1895

Hopkins, a Democrat, was the first of nine Irish-Catholic Chicago mayors. He was a machinist at the Pullman Railcar factory in what is now the Southside of Chicago. In 1888, he started Arcade Trading Company.

He was elected mayor in 1893 by a plurality of 1,220 votes.

His inaugural address of December 27, 1893, can be found in the Chicago City Council minutes. Part of it is reprinted here:

GENTLEMEN OF THE COUNCIL—With deep appreciation of the solemnity of its proceedings, this Council has taken proper action regarding the suddenly created vacancy in the Mayor's office. After an election in which the voters of Chicago manifested deep interest, it is my duty as Mayor-elect formally to enter upon the performance of the assigned task. This I do with unaffected diffidence, but with resolute purpose to meet as far as lies within my power to demands of a situation rendered more difficult because of widespread distress in commercial and industrial affairs. It is my aim to faithfully serve the City of Chicago, and to this end I sincerely and confidentially ask your counsel and assistance.

The corporate authorities of Chicago are the mayor and Common Council. Broadly defined their field is separate. With the Council lies legislative duty; with the mayor the task of executive work. But their relations and duties are closer than indicated by the line usually drawn. They so interweave and blend that they are practically one. I am glad to recognize this unity and to appeal to it in behalf of that sentiment which is common to us all, pride in Chicago's place among the great cities of the world and sincere desire to promote its well-being.

One of our first duties is to perfect a business already entered upon through your direction whereby the finances of the city may be placed in absolute order. You are familiar with that requirement of the law under which the city is incorporated whereby the expenditures of the fiscal year must be regulated strictly in accordance with the provisions of the annual appropriation bill. Money is raised by the city for no other than a corporate purpose, and to divert funds thus raised to other than corporate purposes is manifestly to disregard the law in one of its essentials. In no subdivision of the city government is it proper that expenditures should exceed specific appropriations, and it is important, therefore, that the exact condition of funds in the Treasury should be known at all times in order that the heads of departments may not be betrayed into excess of expenditure. The accounts of the Comptroller's office, wherein the condition of city.

31

CARTER HARRISON JR.
1897–1905
1911–1915

Long before the Daleys, we had the Harrisons. Carter Harrison Jr. served five terms as mayor. This Harrison was the first mayor of Chicago to have been born in Chicago.

Harrison was not a Prohibitionist and supported the freedom to drink. This stance played a big part in his election, making him a popular man with a lot of hard-drinking Chicagoans.

Harrison was a bit of a reformist, as he pushed for the public to have its say through referendums on policy matters. He also advocated a direct primary system, giving the people more of a voice in choosing their leaders.

Harrison brought about the elevated train tracks, a signature feature of Chicago to this day.

Harrison was criticized for not cracking down on vice, so he closed the world-famous Everleigh Club, a renown and extremely upscale and profitable brothel. This silenced his critics who thought he was not tough on vice, but angered the many powerful clients who enjoyed the services this club provided.

32

EDWARD DUNNE
1905–1907

In addition to being elected mayor of Chicago, Dunne also served as governor of Illinois, the only person to hold both offices.

He was a Northwestern Law School graduate, lawyer, and politician. Dunne had thirteen children.

Dunne was a circuit court judge in 1892, was the mayor in 1905, and was elected governor in 1913. Long after serving as governor, in 1933, he was an attorney for the Cook County Board of Elections.

As mayor he was considered quite radical and thought to be a socialist. He fought hard to establish municipal ownership of services such as the transit system, and when he failed, he regulated them as much as he could.

He tried to play the Prohibition issue down the middle, angering both sides that held extreme views on the hot-button topic. In other words, he was a politician.

33

FRED BUSSE
1907–1911

Fred Busse was the son of a Civil War officer and president of the Busse Coal Company. Prior to serving as mayor, he spent time in the state House of Representatives, as a state senator, and as Illinois's treasurer. He also served as postmaster.

He was the first mayor to serve a four-year term due to a change in election laws.

Busse ran as a businessman and was elected, in part, because he successfully convinced the electorate to get government out of the hands of career politicians.

While serving as mayor, he was secretly married.

Prior to coming to Chicago, he made his mark politically in the suburb of North Chicago, where he served as a bailiff and deputy.

34

WILLIAM HALE THOMPSON
1915–1923
1927–1931

"Big Bill" Thompson was the consummate politician. He was extremely ambitious.

As mayor, he enforced "Blue Laws," which closed bars throughout the city. He built a very powerful political machine and hired many civil service workers, alarming good government advocates.

Mindful that Chicago had many Central European immigrants, especially Germans, he was an outspoken advocate of staying out of World War I. He hoped this stance would propel him to a seat in the US Senate, which he ran for while sitting as mayor, but his bid was unsuccessful.

Many suspected he was involved with Al Capone's gang during the time he served as mayor.

35

WILLIAM DEVER
1923–1927

Dever served as an alderman for the Seventeenth Ward for eight years, during which time he developed an excellent reputation as he fought for improved schools, parks, and public works. Beginning in 1910, he served twelve years as a circuit court judge.

Because of his sterling reputation for integrity, he was recruited to run for mayor as a reformer.

He won election and worked quite hard at improving schools and law enforcement in the city. He was responsible for establishing Midway Airport.

A man of integrity, he enforced Prohibition because it was the law, despite not being a Prohibitionist himself. He achieved national acclaim for his actions.

Dever was viewed as an honest and competent reformer.

36

ANTON CERMAK
1931–1933

Cermak is probably best known for being assassinated when he made an appearance with President Franklin Roosevelt. The bullet was most likely meant for FDR. Obviously, Cermak did not complete his term.

Cermak was the first and only foreign-born Chicago mayor. He was originally from Czechoslovakia.

Before entering politics, Cermak worked in coal mines and saloons.

His political experience included a stint in the state legislature, time as an alderman, work as a bailiff, and the presidency of the Cook County Board of Commissioners.

Cermak became Democratic Party chairman and was the consummate politician, especially adept at ethnic politics. He put together ethnic coalitions as a candidate that allowed him to reach City Hall.

37

FRANK CORR
1933

Corr served only twenty-nine days as acting mayor after the assassination of Mayor Cermak.

Originally from Brooklyn, he was a graduate of Chicago's Kent Law School, worked as the assistant Corporation Counsel for Chicago (the city's top lawyer), and was an alderman from the Seventeenth Ward.

Corr died in 1934 just before he was to be sworn in as a circuit court judge.

38

EDWARD KELLY
1933–1947

Long-serving Ed Kelly eventually came to head a powerful political machine. He worked for the Chicago Sanitary District for forty years, eventually rising to chief engineer before entering elective politics.

In 1932, when Chicago suffered its highest unemployment rate ever, Kelly was encouraged to run for mayor to shepherd the city through difficult times. He won.

He cut budgets, oversaw the Century of Progress Exhibition, and enjoyed support from all quarters, business and labor included.

His well-oiled political machine kept humming because his supporters were taken care of.

Kelly was so powerful on the national stage that he was a close advisor of President Roosevelt. FDR sought his advice on many public works projects.

Kelly laid plans for what eventually became the Chicago Transit Authority.

Interparty squabbles and hints of scandal led to him leaving office.

39

MARTIN KENNELLY
1947–1955

Hailing from the Bridgeport neighborhood, Kennelly quit grade school to become a stock boy at Marshall Field's (now Macy's). He eventually became a self-made millionaire. He served as a captain in the army during World War I.

Kennelly was recruited to run for mayor because he was an extraordinarily successful businessman. His lack of political skills, and his distaste for politics, made him a rather ineffectual mayor. Ward bosses and the City Council ran the city during his tenure.

Eventually, the Democratic Party stopped supporting him and backed a mayoral candidate with more political acumen: Richard J. Daley.

40

RICHARD JOSEPH DALEY
1955–1976

It is not too much of a stretch to say Richard Daley was in a gang when he was young. He belonged to a somewhat gang-like group called the Hamburgs. The group morphed into an athletic club of sorts (he was their second baseman) and then became a political group that gave Daley a start in politics.

Daley spoke very much like a blue-collar neighborhood guy from Bridgeport (he was the third Chicago mayor in a row from that Chicago neighborhood), but he was a law school graduate (DePaul). He garbled syntax during his tenure as mayor, and he was often the point of barbs directed his way because of this.

Daley, a nationally prominent Democrat, got his start as a Republican state senator, but that was a decision of convenience to fill a vacancy.

Daley ran a very efficient political machine and was able to have the City Council fall in line most of the time. He used precinct captains effectively in elections, many of which owed his organization their city jobs.

Daley was a kingmaker of sorts; many historians feel he was responsible for delivering Illinois to JFK in the 1960 presidential election.

During Daley's tenure as mayor, O'Hare Airport was built, as was the Sears Tower and the Hancock Building, all iconic Chicago structures.

In 1968, during the riots in the aftermath of the Martin Luther King assassination, Daley gave police a "shoot to kill" order, which, fortunately, was ignored by the police brass. He also was in charge during the 1968 Democratic National Convention in Chicago, where his police force was notoriously violent against antiwar protesters.

Daley's nemesis was Mike Royko, a Chicago newspaper columnist who grilled Daley in his column and wrote a less-than-flattering book about Daley entitled *Boss*.

Daley was known as a family man who attended Mass daily. He is the father of Richard M. Daley, who also was a long-serving mayor of Chicago.

To Daley's credit, he was often grilled by the press but never avoided press conferences. Due to his garbled syntax, it was often difficult for people to understand just what he was saying.

41

MICHAEL BILANDIC
1976–1979

Bilandic succeeded Daley as mayor after the latter died of a heart attack while in office. He got his start in politics being appointed as an alderman by Daley.

Bilandic was appointed interim mayor after Daley's death but lost an election to become mayor in his own right to Jane Byrne, primarily because the city did a terrible job dealing with a major snowstorm.

42

JANE BYRNE
1979–1983

Jane Byre rode the public's dissatisfaction with Bilandic's handling of a snowstorm to the mayor's office.

Prior to being mayor, she served in many city and political positions, most notably the commissioner of consumer sales, where she tried to look out for the rights of consumers.

As mayor, she famously moved into a dangerous public housing complex to draw attention to the needs of the people there and to work on improvements for public housing.

While in office, she married a well-known newspaper writer, and this added a little color to her administration.

Byrne lost reelection in a three-way race to Harold Washington (who became Chicago's first black mayor) and Richard M. Daley (who eventually succeeded the victorious Washington).

43

HAROLD WASHINGTON
1983–1987

Harold Washington was Chicago's first African American mayor and, as a result, was a notable and popular figure nationally and internationally.

His father was a precinct captain as well as a lawyer and minister; his mother was a notable singer. Washington grew up in the Bronzeville neighborhood of Chicago, considered one of the centers of African American culture at the time. He attended Du Sable High School in the city, dropping out because he was bored. He eventually worked in a meat packing plant and for the US Treasury, and he was drafted into World War II, earning the rank of first sergeant. He served in the Pacific Theatre in a segregated unit, helping to build runways.

Returning home after the war, he became actively involved in civil rights issues while attending Roosevelt College (now Roosevelt University); eventually he received a law degree from Northwestern University, where he was among the few black students.

In 1960, he helped found the Chicago League of Negro Voters.

Washington served in the Illinois House of Representatives from 1965 to 1976, the Illinois Senate from 1976 to 1980, and the US House of Representatives from 1980 to 1983. Washington was mayor from 1983 until 1987, when he died in office.

As a US congressman, he helped extend the Voting Rights Act.

As mayor, he received black and Latino support from a City Council that was racially divided. He received little support from white aldermen. His time in office was often described in the press as the "Council Wars" era.

Despite the racial divisions, Washington was able to see many of his priorities enacted. Due to the divisions in the City Council, Mayor Washington often used the power of the veto.

The impressive Washington Library is named after Washington. It is one of the world's most impressive big city libraries.

Washington was generally viewed as a charismatic and hardworking mayor. He was extremely popular with many blacks nationally and overseas because of his personality, and the historic accomplishment of being Chicago's first black mayor.

44

EUGENE SAWYER
1987–1989

After Harold Washington's death, the City Council elected Sawyer, another African American, as acting mayor.

Sawyer ran for mayor in his own right but lost that election to Richard M. Daley, the son of Richard J. Daley.

Sawyer was the perfect man to replace Washington, as his calm demeanor and soft-spoken manner was needed in the contentious "Council Wars" era.

Sawyer enacted many of Washington's programs, including a landmark gay rights ordinance, one of the first in the country.

Sawyer had many unsuccessful business ventures after serving as mayor and was relatively poor when he died.

45

RICHARD MICHAEL DALEY
1989–2011

"Richard the Second" hailed from one of America's most prominent political families. His father was a powerful Chicago mayor, his brother was a Cook County commissioner, and another brother served as the nation's secretary of commerce and as President Obama's chief of staff. Only thirteen years came between the mayoral reigns of the Daleys.

Daley received a law degree from Chicago's DePaul University but did not pass the bar exam on his first try. He became a state senator, and in 1980, he was elected state's attorney for Cook County, running on a platform of stricter enforcement of narcotics laws.

Daley lost the first time he ran for mayor, but he won the second time, beating Eugene Sawyer in the Democratic primary.

As mayor, Daley took control of the public schools, became a strong advocate for gun control, and became a very strong mayor. The City Council generally fell in line.

Famously, he argued with the Federal Aviation Administration, which was promoting an airport on the lakefront. Under the cover of darkness, Daley had the airport bulldozed. It is now a park.

Daley's tenure saw its share of scandals, as well as a failed bid for the Olympics. He also sold off some city assets to private concerns to help the budget, and questions remain as to whether or not the city got the best of those deals.

Daley developed Millennium Park, as well as the Navy Pier, making Chicago an impressive tourist destination.

He is currently a fellow at the University of Chicago and sits on the board of Coca-Cola.

46

RAHM EMANUEL
2011–Present

Rahm, or the "Rahmfather," as some in the press like to call him, truly was a powerful man before becoming mayor. Before leading the city, he was President Obama's chief of staff.

Before serving as chief of staff, Emanuel was a US congressman and advisor to President Clinton.

Emanuel, when younger, studied ballet and turned down a scholarship to the Joffrey Ballet. He also volunteered to serve in the Israeli Self-Defense Force (IDF) during a time of crisis.

One of Emanuel's brothers is a prominent oncologist, and another is a prominent Hollywood agent.

Emanuel faces many challenges as mayor, including severe budget problems and city pension liabilities. He also will have to deal with issues in the public schools.

He had served only a short time as this book was written.

ABOUT THE AUTHOR

Bradley Rasch is a college professor and researcher. He has authored books on presidential trivia and American government. He currently teaches at a Chicago area college and lives with his wife in the Chicago suburbs.